# Canaries

**NIKKI MOUSTAKI**

*Canaries*

*Project Team*
Editor: Tom Mazorlig
Copy Editor: Stephanie Fornino
Indexer: Dianne L. Schneider
Interior Design: Leah Lococo Ltd. and Stephanie Krautheim
Design Layout: Patricia Escabi

*T.F.H. Publications*
President/CEO: Glen S. Axelrod
Executive Vice President: Mark E. Johnson
Publisher: Christopher T. Reggio
Production Manager: Kathy Bontz

T.F.H. Publications, Inc.
One TFH Plaza
Third and Union Avenues
Neptune City, NJ 07753

*Discovery Communications, Inc. Book Development Team*
Marjorie Kaplan, President, Animal Planet Media
Carol LeBlanc, Vice President, Licensing
Elizabeth Bakacs, Vice President, Creative Services
Brigid Ferraro, Director, Licensing
Peggy Ang, Vice President, Animal Planet Marketing
Caitlin Erb, Licensing Specialist

Printed and bound in China
07 08 09 10 11 1 3 5 7 9 8 6 4 2

ISBN 978-0-7938-3795-3

Library of Congress Cataloging-in-Publication Data
Moustaki, Nikki, 1970-
  Canaries / Nikki Moustaki.
    p. cm. – (Animal planet pet care library)
  Includes index.
  ISBN 978-0-7938-3795-3 (alk. paper)
  1. Canaries. I. Title.
SF463.M68 2008
636.6'8625–dc22

2007031059

This book has been published with the intent to provide accurate and authoritative information in regard to the subject matter within. While every reasonable precaution has been taken in preparation of this book, the author and publisher expressly disclaim responsibility for any errors, omissions, or adverse effects arising from the use or application of the information contained herein. The techniques and suggestions are used at the reader's discretion and are not to be considered a substitute for veterinary care. If you suspect a medical problem consult your veterinarian.

*The Leader In Responsible Animal Care For Over 50 Years!*®
www.tfh.com

# Table of Contents

# Chapter 1

# Why I Adore My

# Canary

My first canary was a white mixed breed named Lucky. A friend purchased him for me as a gift. I had kept many parrots and a large variety of finches, but never a canary. I was intrigued by this little bird and wanted to know more about him, so I read everything I could get my hands on about canaries. Eventually, I got another, and then a few more, and then I was in the breeding business— well not really, but I decided that I'd like to try my hand at canary breeding because I had been so successful with breeding parrots. Boy, did I have a lot to learn!

Canaries are beautiful, bright little birds, but they are also finicky and quirky, and they need a patient owner who has a knack for attention to detail. This book will give you some great advice on all aspects of keeping canaries, from housing, accessories, and feeding to health and breeding.

## The Wild Canary

The canary is a domesticated companion bird, unlike other commonly kept birds, like parrots. The canary does occur in the wild, but in captivity the bird is quite different from its wild counterparts. The wild canary (*Serinus canaria*) is a member of the finch family (Fringillidae), a native of the Canary Islands, Madeira, and the Azores. Its name comes from its primary homeland, the Canary Islands, which were actually named after the dogs kept on the island by the natives; this bird, then, is actually named after a fighting dog, probably the Perro de Presa Canario, also called the Canary Dog. There are still an estimated 160,000 to 180,000 wild canaries on the Canary Islands and an estimated 70,000 to 130,000 elsewhere. But those numbers are small in comparison to how many domestic canaries live in homes all across the world.

The wild canary is much smaller than the domestic canary and occurs in one color: a variegated greenish-grayish-yellow, with blackish-brown striations on its wings, back, and flanks. It looks a little like a common sparrow but smaller, and it has a lovely singing voice. There are distinct (though slight) differences between the genders. The coloration of the male is slightly brighter, and he's slimmer than the hen. The wild canary lives primarily in open, arid scrubland.

The wild canary was imported into Europe by the Spaniards as early as the 1400s. Back then, they didn't care much that

*The domestication of canaries began in the 1400's, but they did not become common until much later.*

the bird was a little drab looking—what mattered was its song. By the 1600s, the birds were popular across Europe, especially with royalty, pricing the birds out of reach of commoners. Also, those people involved with breeding the birds sold only the males, which were more desirable because of their singing ability, but the practice of holding back the hens made it even more impossible for the everyday person to have a canary. Eventually, bird fanciers in Italy were able to get hens, and the creation of the domestic canary began in earnest. Soon, canaries were a staple in the homes and shops of Europe.

Over the years, many distinct varieties, or breeds, of canaries have been developed. Some were bred for the way they sing and some for the way they look. These distinctions depended largely on where they were being bred. For example, the British took delight in creating masterful songbirds, and the French, Belgians, and Italians liked to experiment with size, feather type, and posture. There are nearly thirty varieties of canaries bred today. Even the United States has its own canary, the American Singer, developed in the 1930s. There are also "mixed-breed" canaries, those who are crossbred between two (or more) breeds. The mixed-breed is also commonly called the "kitchen canary," which isn't a breed unto itself—it's more like a mutt.

## Canary in the Coal Mine

The first coal mines didn't have adequate ventilation, a sad fact that took the lives of many of the early miners. Because they also didn't have the technology to develop carbon monoxide or methane gas detectors back then, miners did the next best thing: They took small animals into the mines, and when the animals died, it was time to rush outside for some fresh air. Miners typically took mice into the mine but then found that canaries were a lot better. The minute the canary started swaying and then dropped off of its perch—dead—the miners knew that trouble was in the air. The canary has an incredibly delicate respiratory system. A happy singer would keep the miners company all day long with his cheerful song, but when he stopped singing, they used his silence as a potential alarm. Today, the term "canary in a coal mine" is used to indicate any early warning of a potential bad situation.

Canaries also can be successfully bred with other birds, such as the house finch, bullfinch, siskin, twite, goldfinch, linnet, serin, and chaffinch. These birds are usually called "mules" because they are often infertile, but sometimes they are fertile and can be bred together to create new varieties of canary. Crossbreeding like this is sometimes done to create a superior singing bird or to experiment with color. Actually, most canaries are descended from crosses such as these, which were done early in the canary's evolution.

*There are many different breeds of canary. This is a Red Factor American Singer.*

## Physical Characteristics

The domestic canary ranges in size from 4 to 8 inches (10 to 20.3 cm) and weighs between 12 and 30 grams (0.4 and 1 oz, although birds are usually measured in grams because of their small size). Each "breed" has a different manner of singing or of appearance. Canaries are broken down into three categories: song, type, and color. Here's a short breakdown of the three categories.

## The Song Canaries

The song canaries are bred to sing well, and each breed has a different way of singing, with different notes and patterns. Here are details about the most popular song canaries.

### American Singer Canary

This hardy little canary was developed by eight women in the Boston area in the 1930s by crossing the Roller and the Border canaries. The women wanted to create a canary with a louder song than the Roller, and with more variation. Unlike the other song canaries, there are no specific songs, sounds, or notes that the American Singer needs to know or sing to win in competitions or be considered a good singer. Rather, he is judged on how often he sings, his volume (should be medium), the length of his song, his tone, tempo, and creativity, among other things.

# Types of Feathers

Canaries have a variety of types of feathers that make up their beautiful plumage. Here are a few:

**Bristle:** The stiff, protective bristle feathers are found on the face and near the mouth.

**Contour:** These are the feathers found on every part of the bird except the face and legs. The majority of a contour feather is colored, but the base is usually white or pale and downy, helping to insulate the bird.

**Down:** These white, downy, insulating feathers grow close to the skin, under the contour feathers.

**Filoplume:** The filoplume feathers are very fine and have just a few barbs (feather structures) on the end. These are attached to nerve endings and used to help the bird sense the position of his feathers in flight and when preening.

**Flight:** The flight feathers grow on the wings and the tail. They are stiffer than contour feathers and are uneven on either side of the vane (the shaft that runs through the feather). They do not have down at the base like the contour feathers do.

**Powder down:** As these down feathers grow, the sheath that protects them crumbles into a fine powder, which the bird spreads throughout his feathers while preening. This powder helps to waterproof the bird.

**Semiplume:** Semiplume feathers are softer than contour feathers but not as soft as down feathers. They grow on the body with the contour feathers and offer the bird some insulation.

The American Singer is a great choice for beginners to canaries.

### Belgian Waterslager Canary

The Belgian Waterslager (also called the Malinois) was developed in Belgium in the early 1700s. Its trademark sounds include "water notes" (bubbling and water drops) and bell and flute sounds, and it is known for a wide variety of notes in its songs. Physically, the Waterslager is yellow in color and is approximately 6.5 inches (16.5 cm) in length; it can have "ticking," or variegation in a darker color, on less than 25 percent of its body. Some Waterslagers are white, but these are said to have come from cross breeding with other types of canaries. For this breed (or any of the song canary breeds) to stay true to their songs, they must be kept only with others of their own breed, or else their song can become corrupted as they learn other notes and tours (variation on set of notes).

When Waterslagers are shown, they are judged and awarded points largely on the various types of notes they produce (which all have phonetic names), as well as the timbre, volume, and quality of the sounds. Points are also deducted for undesirable sounds (which also have phonetic names). Note that canary enthusiasts make a firm distinction between the Belgian Waterslager and the Dutch, most notably in the differences between the songs.

### German Roller Canary

The German Roller, also known as the Hartz Roller, was developed in the 1700s in Germany. Its main characteristic is that it sings with the beak closed, making its song soft and lovely. People show these birds in what is essentially a singing contest, with specific songs that a team of birds must

## The Red Siskin

The Venezuelan black-hooded red siskin is in the finch family (like the canary) and is the species responsible for the red gene in Red Factor canaries. As early as the 13th century, Spanish bird breeders were crossing the siskin and the canary to create a unique pet. Unlike Red Factor canaries, however, the red siskin does not need color food to retain its vibrant hues. This species is also an accomplished singer, with a sweet, melodic voice. Unfortunately, this bird has been so sought after, both as a cage bird and to have its feathers adorn ladies' hats, that it has been nearly decimated in its native habitat. Today, the American Federation of Aviculture's Red Siskin Project is attempting to bring back the population, at least in captivity.

*The Waterslager is renowned for bubbling, liquid sounds in its song.*

know and sing well to win, with the breed's trademark sounds of rolls and flutes.

### Russian Singer

In the 1700s, canary keepers in Moscow brought in canaries from Germany and soon noticed that these exceptional songsters reproduced the songs of wild birds very easily. These canaries founded the line that has become the Russian Singer. This is a rare variety of canary, that is probably unavailable in the United States. At first glance, its looks are less than distinctive, but its melodic song is what defines this breed. Even though collectors prize its unique song, it has unfortunately not traveled far from its home country.

### Spanish Timbrado Canary

The Spanish Timbrado is as close to its wild cousins as any of the song canaries,

though it wasn't made "official" until breeders in Spain in the 1940s and 50s took up its cause. They come in green, yellow, white, variegated, and cinnamon. Its song is cheerful and reminiscent of Spanish castanets.

## The Type Canaries

Type canaries are bred for how they look. Here's a rundown of the most popular type canaries.

### Belgian Fancy Canary

The Belgian Fancy is "bird of position," but it is also a "frilled" breed. This is a long, thin bird that stands in a hunched position, which looks somewhat uncomfortable and awkward. It was developed in the 1800s and has roots in the Yorkshire and Scotch canaries. This is not a great bird for beginners to the fancy because it tends to be high strung and doesn't breed as easily as some of the more common breeds. It is

## Feather Types

Canary feathers are termed either "hard" or "soft." (Soft-feathered birds are also called "buff.") Hard-feathered birds have bright colors and shiny, tight feathers. Soft-feathered birds have more gentle colors and downier plumage. In general, breeders try to breed hard-feathered and soft-feathered birds together. Sometimes, when soft-feathered birds are bred together, the babies can have feather issues, including feather lumps—ingrown feathers. The hard feather is also called "intensive," and the soft feather is called "nonintensive."

### Fife Canary

Fife canaries began in the 1950s in Scotland to bring the Border canary back to its original form. It is smaller than today's Border and has become a popular breed. It comes in a variety of color mutations. This is one of the easier canaries for a beginner to breed.

### The Frills

The "frilled" canaries look a little like feather dusters, with soft, sweeping feathers all over the body, giving the bird a stout, puffy look that can be quite elegant. The Parisian Frill Canary is one of the commonly kept frilled breeds. It's a large breed with feather frills all over its face, head, and body; it also features twisted toes, which isn't a fault in this breed.

Other frilled breeds include the Dutch Frill, Gibber Italicus, Giboso Espanol, Hunchback Frill, Makige Frill, Japanese Frill, Melado Tenerife, Munich Frill, Southern Frill, Swiss Frill, Giant Italian Frill, Mehringer, Milano Frill, Northern Frill, Florin, and Padovan or Paduan Crested Frill.

similar to the Gibber Italicus and Giboso Espanol, which are even more frilled and strangely hunched over.

### Border Canary

The Border canary is what everyone imagines when they picture a canary—a robust, lively little bird, usually found in yellow, with a rounded head and chest. It is bred to be small, at around 5 inches (12.7 cm) in length, and should stand at a 60-degree angle on the perch. It is from the north of England and the Scottish borders and was developed in the 1700s. It comes in many color varieties.

### Gloster Canary

The little Gloster canary is a crested breed with a hairdo that looks a little like Ringo Starr's 1960's mop. The individuals with the crest are called coronas, and the individuals without the crest are called consorts. The breed was developed around the 1920s in Gloucestershire, England. Two crested birds should never be bred together, which is why the consorts are so important, even though they don't have the characteristic Gloster corona. The crested gene is dominant and will cause 25 percent of the young to die, usually in the shell or just after hatching. This is called a "lethal gene." Instead, crested birds should be bred to consorts, usually a crested hen to a consort male.

## Lizard Canary

This is probably the oldest variety of canary, and it is increasing in popularity after some shaky times in its history. World War II essentially decimated this breed, but just a few dozen pairs brought it back to a substantial number. It is prized for the spangled, textured look to its feathers, giving it a scaly appearance—hence its name.

## Norwich Canary

At 6.5 inches (16.5 cm) tall, this popular canary is stocky and much larger and thicker than some of the other commonly kept canaries. It comes in a variety of color mutations and can be "color fed," meaning that the bird's feathers will take on the color of an additive to the food or water, making the bird a bright shade

The Border canary shows a range of colors. It is one of the smaller breeds.

## Canary Life Span

A properly cared for canary can live to be more than ten years old. In general, breeding hens live the shortest amount of time, perhaps as little as five years. Breeding males live to perhaps ten years of age. Very pampered pet birds can live well over 10 years, and anecdotal reports tell of canaries living to be 20!

of orange or red. This breed was developed in the late 1800s in Norwich, England.

### Scotch Fancy Canary

The Scotch Fancy breed began in the early 1800s and is a "bird of position," meaning that it stands in a particular posture. It has a "snaky" head and long, tapering neck and is close to 7 inches (17.8 cm) in length. It stands as if it's raising itself up to look at something far away, its body shaped almost like the letter "C." It became scarce in bird circles for a while, but it's coming back.

### Stafford Canary

The Stafford is another crested breed. In this breed, the crested birds are called simply "crested," and the birds without the crest are called "noncrested." The Stafford was created in the late 1980s, and in 1990 the Stafford Canary Club gained membership in the Canary Counsel of Great Britain. The breed soon became popular in the United States. It occurs in a variety of color mutations.

### Yorkshire Canary

This large canary is close to 7 inches (17.8 cm) in length and comes in a variety of color mutations. The breed, developed in the 1840s, is sometimes color fed. The primary characteristic of the Yorkshire is its stance (it's another "bird of position"), which the standard says should be a "fearless carriage, legs long without being stilty, and slight lift of tail."

*There are several different breeds of frilled canaries, all with wispy, swirled feathers. Some of these are challenging to breed.*

## The Color Canaries

There are hundreds of color mutations in the canary, often with very slight distinctions to the novice eye. Here are just a few of the color variations.

### Ground Colors

Canaries are considered to come in a handful of "ground" colors, which are altered by various mutations. Ground colors include yellow, white, rose, and red. The colors are changed by additions to the feathers, such as an overall suffusion of another color (like brown) or just a small addition of color in a few feathers.

### -Ino

The "ino" is a suffix tacked on to the mutation it refers to, such as lutino (clear yellow), rubino (clear red), and albino (clear white). All of these birds have red eyes, pink feet, and a lack of the pigment melanin in their feathers. The "ino" mutation is sex-linked recessive; the "ino" gene is carried on the X chromosome. Males have two Xs and females have one. Hens always show "ino" if they carry it in their genes, but cocks can hide the "ino" gene on the other X chromosome. This can help to determine the gender of clutches of chicks; for example, all of the "ino" babies in a clutch will be hens if the mother is not an "ino" but the father is.

### Melanin

Melanin is the chemical that gives feathers their dark brown and black pigments. Melanin expresses itself in most of the canary mutations and expresses itself by making all or some of the feathers dark. For example, a Red Factor melanin canary will be dark red, while a Red Factor lipochrome canary will be a light or bright red.

### Mosaic

The Mosaic gene creates visual differences between the genders. The coloring of the bird (usually red, orange, or yellow) occurs in patches. The female Mosaic mutation has broader, softer feathers than the male and has little color in the face compared to the male. Mosaics occur in lipochrome, where the feather patterns are the most dramatic, and melanin, creating a white bird with gray or light brown markings.

### Red Factor

The Red Factor canary is a pale peach or orange when it's hatched, and it owes this original color to the red siskin, whose genes were introduced to the canary line in the late 1920s. Most Red Factors are color fed with special pigmented foods and water additives, creating a bird that is a deep orange or red. Don't try to feed any other canaries this color food—only the

*The pattern on the Lizard canary gives it a somewhat scaly appearance.*

## Suitability as a Child's Pet

The canary makes a nice child's pet if he is kept as a family bird and has an adult in charge of his feeding, cleaning, and care. You can tell your child that the canary is hers, but she shouldn't be responsible for much, if any, of the bird's care until the child is old enough to consistently do her chores without being asked. Because a canary is usually a "watching only" bird, he will probably spend most of his time in a cage or aviary. If you intend to let the canary have free flight in the house (as many people do), the household should not contain children, who are apt to leave a door or window open without thinking of the bird. A child might prefer a pet that she can handle, like a parakeet, hamster or a puppy.

Red Factor (and a small handful of other color-bred canaries) has the genetic predisposition to change color when color fed.

### Yellow (Lipochrome)

This typical canary color is created by carotenoids deposited in the feather called lipochromes, which are also responsible for red and orange birds. Yellow lipochrome birds maintain their color by ingesting seeds, but red and orange birds must ingest beta carotene, canthaxanthin, or other colored chemicals to keep their color vibrant.

## Taming Canaries

Most canaries are considered "watching only" companions, but some can

*The Scotch Fancy canary stands in an odd, elongated manner.*

become very tame if you take the time to earn their trust. If you want a tame canary, you're probably going to have to breed him yourself. It's doubtful that the canaries at the pet shop or even at the breeder's home are going to be tame or have the ability to be tamed. They have already imprinted on other birds and are going to be fearful of close contact with you. If you're

in the nest. As they fledge out, handle them gently until they eventually become used to your touch. If you feed them from your hand, you'll find that they will be happy to perch on your finger or

*The Gloster canary is one of the crested breeds.*

really gentle and patient, you can train your canary to take food from your hand, kind of like how you might lure a wild squirrel to take a peanut from you.

If you do breed your canaries and want to tame the chicks, wait until they are about a week old, and if the parents allow it, you can start to pet them gently

shoulder as you do your household chores. But don't get ahead of yourself—this is the exception, not the rule.

## Temperament and Behavior

Canaries can be bossy and territorial with one another, but with humans they can be shy and even friendly. They are not social birds and prefer to live alone. However, during breeding season, if you "condition" your birds to want to mate (more on that in Chapter 6), they will want to pair up and will make nests and have young. Then, once breeding season is over, they will want their space again.

## Do You Need a Pair?

Unless you're going to breed canaries, you only need one canary per household or per cage. Canaries are the "lone wolves" of the bird world; they actually prefer to be alone. They are extremely territorial, especially the males, and will squabble with and even injure other birds in their territory. Even male/female pairs will fight outside of breeding season. To make your canary comfortable, don't try to offer him a friend, thinking that he's lonely. Instead, leave the radio or television on for him and let him be a part of the bustle of family life. If you keep more than one canary in a room, you risk losing the song of at least one of them, especially if you keep males near hens. Males sing to claim their territory and to get a mate. If you surround your male with hens, he doesn't need to sing anymore. If you put another male nearby, only the more dominant male will sing. Keeping two or more females together is generally okay.

*In the Gloster canary breed, birds without crests are called consorts.*

## Teaching Your Canary to Sing

Yes, male canaries actually need to be taught to sing! Really, what they need is a good tutor singing nearby that they can mimic. Canary breeders will often keep stellar singers near young males to teach them how to sing well from the beginning. Research has shown that canaries who were raised not hearing any song were able to pick up computer-generated song patterns well.

Researchers tried to distort the syntax of the traditional canary song, and the young canaries picked this up as well but then reverted to natural song patterns when it was time to woo a hen or sing to their young. If you're breeding canaries and want your youngsters to learn how to sing well, pick up a canary CD or keep a masterful singer nearby. Canaries are adept mimics— you might be surprised to hear some household noises, like a ringing cell phone, included with the traditional notes of the song. Also of note is the distinction between "rollers" and "choppers." Rollers sing softly with their beak closed, and choppers sing loudly with their beak open.

## Summing Up

In general, your canary should be active and lively, interested in his food and toys, and bathe regularly. If you have a male, he should sing when he's not molting. When he's feeling well, he will sleep and rest on one leg, not two, and he will preen himself almost incessantly. If you keep your canary in a spacious cage, offer the appropriate food and accessories, change the water frequently, and manage the proper type and amount of lighting, he should live a long and happy life.

*Canaries are territorial birds and will often fight if kept together.*

# Boys and Girls

Only male canaries sing, and because singing is one of the primary reasons that most people want a canary, choosing a male is of utmost importance. The problem is that in most breeds, it's nearly impossible to tell the males from the females. A good breeder will know how to tell the genders apart by closely watching and listening to a group of young birds. A conscientious breeder will separate the genders and sell them to stores as individuals with the best educated guess possible. Nevertheless, breeders do make mistakes, so your potential singing male might just lay an egg! If he turns out to be a she, many breeders will exchange the bird for you. If you've bought your bird from a pet shop, you might be out of luck. But don't fret; even though you won't get any elaborate songs from your hen, she'll still be a sweet and cute companion.

# Chapter 2

# The Stuff of

# Everyday Life

Once you have your canary or have decided to add one or more of them to your family, you have to consider all of the accessories that your new bird will need, including proper housing. You'll also have to consider where to place the bird, how to bird-proof your home for his safety, and how and when to clean the cage to keep his environment hygienic. This chapter gives you the lowdown on everything you need to keep your canary content.

## Your Canary's Housing

It's typical to think of a canary in a small cage. Remember Tweety, Sylvester the cat's cartoon nemesis? His famous song lyrics were: "Oh, I'm just a bird in a gilded cage." But Tweety was an exceptional canary, and every time his owner left the house, he'd simply open his cage door and roam around the house, tormenting the cat. Your canary might torment your cat just by his presence in the house, but he certainly isn't going to be able to leave his cage for a little bit of exercise. This means that your canary's cage has to be as spacious as possible to give him the room he needs to stay fit. The days of keeping birds in tiny birdcages are over. Today, birdkeepers know that all birds need space to fly. After all, birds in the wild aren't confined. Canaries who are kept in small cages often become obese, which can greatly reduce their life span.

Whether you're getting a one-canary cage or building an aviary, stick with a square or rectangular cage rather than a round one. Also, choose a cage that's wider than it is tall; unlike parrots, who can climb around cage bars, your canary will only hop or fly from perch to perch, so he needs room to do that.

## The Birdcage

If you have one canary who you're going to keep somewhere in your home inside of a cage,

*Cages are available in numerous sizes and styles. For a canary, select a fairly large cage that is longer than it is tall.*

choose the largest cage that suits your budget and space. This type of cage is often called a "flight cage." There are two kinds of large cages: those made for small birds and those made for large birds. The one made for small birds will have thin bars that are spaced closely together. If the bar spacing is too wide, a small bird may get his head caught between the bars, like a kid with his head between the bars of a banister.

The cage should be made of metal or a combination of metal and plastic. You also can opt for an acrylic cage that reduces mess on your floor, but you have to keep it dry and clean because moisture can build up in a cage that doesn't have adequate ventilation. Metal cages should not include decorative scrollwork, which can catch a toe or wing. Opt for a simpler cage. Also, make sure that the bars are evenly spaced, not tapered toward the top. Avoid wooden cages because wood can become moist and harbor bacteria.

The floor of the cage should ideally have a removable grate, usually made of metal. If it doesn't have a grate, your canary will be able to get to his waste, which isn't healthy. If the cage you get doesn't have a grate, clean the cage more often.

## The Aviary

The canary is well suited to an aviary housing a colony of birds as long as the

FAMILY-FRIENDLY TIP

## Adult Supervision Required

Canaries aren't typically companions for children, but if you do have a child in the house, do not make feeding and caring for the bird one of her chores. Sure, a responsible child may take wonderful care of a bird, but there might come a day when the child forgets or doesn't have time to feed the bird. So that she doesn't get in trouble, the child might not tell an adult that she has forgotten the bird, and days may go by—with disastrous results. If you have a bird—any type of bird—the adults in the home should be the primary caretakers. If you do allow your kids to care for your bird, supervise them.

aviary is large enough to prevent territorial squabbles. If you're going to use an aviary, house just one male with a few females, or more than three males with several females. Two males will quibble, often viciously, over the females, but more than three males seems to be the recipe for relative peace. Canaries also can be kept with other peaceable birds, including

# Canary Cage Checklist

Bird cages come in a bewildering variety of sizes and styles. Only a small number of these are suitable for canaries. The following list will help you select the perfect home for your little companion.

- Is the cage spacious enough for a canary? Ideally, the bird should have plenty of room to fly.
- Do the cage bars taper at any point in the cage (especially on a round cage)? Does the cage have any complicated scrollwork or other decorative touches? Your canary can easily catch and break a toe on cages with this kind of construction.
- What is the cage material? Forgo wood for safer metals, like powder-coated steel and stainless steel.
- Does the tray have a grate over an easily removable tray? The canary should not be able to get to his waste.
- Is the construction of the cage sturdy in general?
- Are the doors so large that you won't be able to service the cage without letting the bird out? Even if you have a very large cage, it should have smaller doors built into the larger doors.
- Does the cage have adequate food and water dishes? Some cages have the feeding and watering stations on the bottom of the cage, which isn't recommended. You'll have to purchase other cups to hang higher in the cage.
- Does the cage come with adequate perches? It's likely that you're going to have to purchase additional perches of various sizes, diameters, and materials.

budgies, cockatiels, some of the grass keets, and some varieties of nonaggressive finches, as long as the aviary is large enough, If you do house birds of various species together, keep a close eye on them, especially the hookbills (budgies, cockatiels, and keets), to make sure that no one terrorizes the other birds' nesting or roosting areas. Even though they are similar in size, never keep lovebirds with canaries. If you're serious about breeding canaries, forget about trying to do it in an aviary setting.

For a colony of birds, make sure that you include an excess of high roosting areas as well as feeding stations. You want to make sure that even the weaker personalities are able to eat, drink, and find a safe and comfortable place to sleep. Also, make sure that there's plenty of shelter from inclement weather. Most outdoor aviaries have a shelter area made of wood that serves as both protection and a place for nighttime roosting.

Canaries who are kept outside all year can become acclimated to the cold and won't mind winter weather if they're able to get out of the wind. Some people equip their aviaries with heated areas to make sure that the birds are comfortable. If it gets really cold where you live, keep thick plastic sheets and warm blankets on hand to cover the aviary walls when the weather gets fierce. Also, make sure that the birds' water doesn't freeze. If you live in a very warm climate, make sure that part of your aviary is shaded all day, and offer your birds plenty of fresh water.

If you have the time and inclination, plant your aviary with safe trees and plants, and create water features

*It is crucial that the spacing of the cage bars is not so great that it allows your canary to push his head out—and possibly get it stuck.*

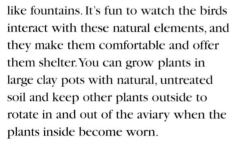

## The Home-Alone Canary

**Because canaries aren't "hands-on" birds, they aren't going to get the same kind of separation anxiety that parrots might have, but they certainly will become bored if there's not enough to do or enough stimulation in their surroundings.**

**Keeping your canary entertained while you're out of the house is pretty easy. First, leave the radio or television on while you're gone. Choose a radio station that plays classical music or that has talk shows on all day, and keep the volume at a moderate to low level. For the television, a station like Animal Planet would be ideal. For a bird, noise means safety. In the wild, a noisy environment means that there are no predators nearby; everyone is just going about their business. Even though your canary is pretty removed from the wild, he still has instincts that tell him that dead quiet means danger is lurking. Once you've decided on a station that your bird likes, invest in some simple toys to place around the cage. Usually, canaries like toys that parakeets like, especially those that include mirrors and small moving parts and bells. Canaries also appreciate "preening" toys—*toys* made of floss or feathers that your canary can preen.**

like fountains. It's fun to watch the birds interact with these natural elements, and they make them comfortable and offer them shelter. You can grow plants in large clay pots with natural, untreated soil and keep other plants outside to rotate in and out of the aviary when the plants inside become worn.

The floor of the aviary can be elevated so that the waste and excess food fall through, or you can use a concrete slab for easy cleaning. Some people prefer natural soil, sand, or a gravel substrate floor, which the birds do enjoy, but the aviary must have adequate drainage.

For safety, the outdoor aviary should be double-wired with screening in between the wires. The space between the wires prevents predators from reaching into the aviary and pulling your birds through the wires—yes, it can happen! The double wiring also prevents contact with wild birds that will want to feed inside your aviary, possibly passing disease to your birds. In addition, the screening prevents mosquitoes and other pests from entering your aviary and infecting your birds with illnesses.

### Building a Cage

If you're even slightly handy, you can build your canary a nice safe cage. It might not look perfect if you're not a carpenter, but I can tell you how to do it so that it's cheap, large, and easy.

Here are some simple directions:

1. Go to a feed store and buy a J-tool and some J-clips. Ask someone at the store to teach you how to use the tool. It couldn't be easier. The tool can be a little hard on your hands, so buy some work or gardening gloves, too. While you're there, buy door fasteners as well. (They'll know what you need.) You also will need a small wire clipper.

2. At the hardware store (or feed store), buy a roll of 1/4-inch (0.6 cm) hardware cloth. This is your cage wire.

3. When you get home, take the hardware cloth outside and hose it down thoroughly. Then, spray it liberally with white vinegar and scrub it vigorously with a stiff copper or metal brush. Most hardware cloth is galvanized against rust which means that it has a coating of zinc on it, and zinc is toxic to birds.

4. Leave the hardware cloth outside in the elements for about two weeks, repeating the vinegar scrub and hose-down every couple of days. Now you're ready to assemble your cage.

5. Drag the end of the hardware cloth to a place in the wire as large as you want the cage to be—you're making a large round or oval cage. (These shapes are the easiest if you've never done it before.) Clip the end of the wire using the J-tool and J-clips to the spot you've chosen. Now you have a round

*If you have the space, an outdoor aviary makes a great canary home, especially if you wish to have multiple canaries.*

# Bird-Proofing the Home

Because a canary doesn't generally get free roaming privileges in a household, you won't have to do the kind of bird-proofing you would have to do for a parrot, but there are still a few things you must do to make your home safe. Some canaries are allowed to fly free in parts of a household, so if this is the case with your bird, take all the following precautions:

- A household that has birds in it, no matter where they live in the home, should not have any kind of nonstick cookware in use. The nonstick coating emits a lethal vapor when it's heated that kills birds on the spot, especially birds as sensitive as canaries. For the same reason, don't use a self-cleaning oven, a space heater, blow dryer, air popper, or anything else that contains nonstick elements near your bird.
- If your canary is going to have access to your window garden, make sure that all of the plants are nontoxic.

- All windows and doors in the house should have intact screens. If your canary is allowed to fly free, make sure that everyone in the household knows not to open the windows.
- Either cover all mirrors and large picture windows, or leave them dirty. Your canary won't know the difference between a mirror or window and open space, and he may try to fly into it. If the glass surfaces are dirty or you place stickers on them, he will be able to see that they are solid. This is a great excuse not to do windows!
- Make sure that your canary's cage is sturdy so that your dog or cat won't be able to knock it over. If you have a ferret, the bird and this fuzzy predator must never meet—that will be Tweety's last day! Canaries don't mix well with other small mammals or reptiles, either.
- No smoking! Ban smoking inside the house—it's toxic to birds.
- Remove all ceiling fans if your canary is allowed to fly free in your home, or at least tape over the switches so that they can't be turned on accidentally while the bird is out.
- Remove or cover all halogen lamps if your canary is allowed to fly free. You will have a sizzled bird if he decides to land there.

wire circle with no top or bottom.

6. Using the rest of the wire or a new roll, lay a flat piece of wire over the top of your circle so that it overlaps the whole thing by about 3 inches (8 cm), give or take. (This isn't an exact science.) J-clip the flat piece to the top of the circle.

7. Flip the circle over and do the same thing to the other end.

8. Now you have a cage that looks like a circle with two square pieces overlapping each end. Flip the thing onto one side, and lay a piece of wire over the ends of the squares and clip it to them.

9. Keep flipping it until you've clipped four flat pieces of wire onto each side of your circle.

10. Now you have a circular cage within a square cage. Pick a side that you like and cut a square hole into the center of it, about 6 x 6 inches (15 x 15 cm), maybe a little more depending on the size of your cage.

11. Next, cut a smaller square out of the circular part of the cage—you have a door within a door.

12. Cut squares of wire a few inches (cm) larger than your door hole squares, and clip them onto the

left side of the door holes, respectively. Clip the door fasteners to the right side of the doors so that they close flush. You may need two fasteners per door.

13. Your cage is double-wired and safe to keep outside. Place the cage onto two hobbyhorses or another type of stand, and place it beneath a covered area so that it's safe from the weather.

14. Add perches, food and water dishes, and toys, and you're set to keep a few canaries!

## Housing Placement

If your canary is going to live inside your home, keep him in a room that's going to get some activity, like a family room or living room. The room where everyone watches television, for example, is a great area for your bird. Don't house him in the garage, bathroom, or kitchen, places that are prone to fumes and temperature changes. Also, don't house him in a child's room, where he may be inundated with too much activity while the child is home or not enough activity while the child is at school.

Ideally, the cage will be on a sturdy and freestanding base or placed onto a sturdy piece of furniture. You also can hang the bird's cage from the ceiling with a chain, but don't place the cage onto a hanging stand, which can be toppled easily by another pet. Place the bird at chest height or higher; birds get nervous when they're too low because they can't keep an eye out for predators.

Place the cage against one wall rather than have it standing or hanging out in the open. The wall gives the bird a measure of security. If you'd rather have the cage out in the open, cover one or more sides of the cage with a solid material, like wood or heavy cloth.

*Place your canary's cage in a room that gets a lot of activity, like the living room or family room.*

*If your canary is allowed out of his cage, you will need to keep a close eye on him.*

The bird should be within "bird's eye view" of a window but shouldn't be up against the window. What your canary sees out the window might frighten him, and he won't be able to get away from what he perceives as a life-threatening danger, like a cat on the windowsill. Also, if the window is flooded with sunlight, your canary may become overheated, or the area around the window might be drafty and become too cold in the wintertime. Finally, there's a chance that someone might see your bird through the window and try to steal him.

Some people dedicate an entire room in their home to their birds, known as the "bird room." The bird room is usually well ventilated and equipped with HEPA filters. The paint on the walls in the bird room should be fresh, nontoxic, and free from chipping, especially if the birds are going to be flying free. Windows should have double screens to make sure that your birds don't get out and to ensure that predators have a hard time coming in. Tile floor is a good idea in a bird room, but you can use pine wood chips that you sweep up each week as they become soiled.

## Housing Accessories

Once you've situated your cage or aviary, it's time to equip your bird's housing with all the things he needs to be well fed, healthy, and entertained.

## Food and Water Bowls

Food and water dishes for birds are often called "coop cups." Your cage will probably come with a couple of plastic or metal cups. Stainless steel is the ideal material for coop cups because it's easy to scrub and disinfect. Plastic can become scratched, and bacteria can grow in the crevices.

It's typical to feed and water canaries with tube-style or on-demand cups, but these can become dirty and clogged if you don't service them regularly. Hooded feeders prevent a lot of mess, but make sure that your canary understands that there's food beneath the hood before you remove the other feeder. If he doesn't know how to use the feeder, he'll likely starve.

If you want your floor to remain relatively seed-free, invest in a perch/cup combo. This is a food cup placed at the end of a long perch so that the cup isn't right against the cage bars. This way, when your canary goes searching for his favorite seed at the bottom of the cup, he will spill the seed into the cage tray rather than onto the floor.

*Partially enclosed bird baths help reduce the mess caused by your happily splashing canary.*

Hanging veggies and millet spray is easy with simple clothespins. Unlike a parrot, a canary is unlikely to get his beak caught in the clothespins, so they're pretty safe to use. Use clips on the outside of the cage only.

## Bird Bath

Canaries love to bathe. They will bathe in the water dish, but it's better if you offer a daily bath in a flat, shallow dish. You can use the clay or plastic dish that goes beneath a flower pot, or even a clean ashtray, or get a shallow bathing dish from your local pet shop. You also can find a type of enclosed bath that hangs from the cage's door. This type is nice because it keeps the water contained so that the rest of the cage doesn't get too damp.

## Toys

It's not typical for a canary to need a lot of toys, but in my experience, the average canary will enjoy certain types of toys, spending good portions of the day ringing a small bell or pecking at a mirror. The types of toys made for parakeets are generally suitable for canaries, especially the plastic toys. You can forgo the wooden chewing toys because canaries won't use them. Instead, opt for toys that incorporate mirrors, bells, bright and shiny objects, and moving parts. Make sure that the toys you include are made for small birds. A toy that's too large can pose a danger to little toes and may even be a choking hazard if the bird gets his head stuck in a ring.

Don't forget swings! Canaries love to swing, so include a few swings in a variety of sizes and materials.

## Perches

Your canary should have a variety of perches to promote foot heath, just like you need a variety of shoes. If you wore the same pair of shoes all day, every day, eventually your feet, posture, and gait would suffer. It's the same for birds. Also, their feet can become sore and raw from touching the same places every day. Try the following types of perches.

### Plastic

Plastic perches aren't the best, so don't use them to the exclusion of other types, although they are easy to clean and last a long time.

### Rope

Perches made from rope come in a variety of sizes, and many of them bend to fit the shape of your cage. Just keep an eye on fraying rope, and cut all loose ends before they can wind around a neck or leg.

### Sand and Concrete

Textured perches are great for keeping the toenails in shape, and birds love to swipe their beak back and forth on these perches to keep it conditioned. Canaries often like to sleep on textured perches, so place them high in the cage toward the back.

### Sandpaper

Do not use the sandpaper sheathes that are often sold

## Homemade Toys

Canaries don't need a lot of toys, but they do appreciate something to do. You don't have to spend a fortune on toys for your bird. Here are directions for making an entertaining toy that my canaries love. You will need a thick plastic coat hanger, sisal twine, and some plastic shirt buttons.

1. Wrap the sides and bottom of the hanger haphazardly with the sisal twine, stopping now and then to make knots in it. There's no right or wrong way to do it; just make sure to wrap it pretty well. The idea is that your canary will be able to grip the hanger without issue.
2. When you're done wrapping, tie 3- to 5-inch (7.5- to 13-cm) lengths of sisal twine all over the hanger so that they're dangling down.
3. On each dangle, tie a plastic button.
4. Add the hanger to your bird's cage or bird room.

Voilà! You have a cheap, easy toy/perch for your canary that should keep him entertained. If you'd like, you can use some of the twine dangles to tie on millet sprays or lettuce leaves. Replace the sisal when it becomes soiled.

# Toxic Plants

The following plants contain one or more parts that are toxic or that are considered an irritant to pets:

aloe
amaryllis
anthurium
apricot kernel
azalea
caladium
calla lily
Chinese evergreen
colchicum
daffodil
dieffenbachia
dumb cane
Easter lily
elephant's ear
English ivy
fishtail palm
holly berry
hyacinth
iris
Jerusalem cherry
lantana
lily of the valley
mistletoe
mountain laurel
oleander
philodendron
ranunculus
rosary pea
sago palm
schefflera
spathiphyllum

The following plants are considered safe to keep around pets:

African daisy
African violet
aluminum plant
baby's tears
golden bamboo
bird's nest fern
Boston fern
camellia
cast iron plant
Christmas cactus
coleus
donkey's tail
dracaena
echeveria
geranium
goldfish plant
ice plant
impatiens
jade plant
Japanese aralia
kalanchoe
lipstick plant
maidenhair fern
nerve plant
Norfolk island pine
orchids (*Cattleya, Epidendrum, Oncidium*)
palms (except for the fishtail palm)
peperomia
prayer plant
purple passion plant
sensitive plant
spider plant
Surinam cherry
Swedish ivy
wax Plant
zebra Plant

in pet shops. These are not only abrasive on the feet, but they can become moist and soiled easily.

### Wooden

Perches come in a variety of different woods, from pine to manzanita to cholla wood. Choose naturally shaped wavy, gnarled wooden perches that have some texture to them. Unlike parrots, canaries don't chew on the wood, so your perches will last a long time.

## Cage Substrate

The bottom of the cage (the tray) needs to be covered with an easily removable substrate so that you can clean the cage in a snap. There are quite a few products on the market today that are sold for this purpose,

*Natural wood perches provide needed exercise for your canary's feet.*

but they are a waste of money, and some can even be harmful. The best, cheapest, and most tidy substrate is plain old newspaper. It's highly absorbent, and the newsprint contains chemicals that actually prevent bacteria growth. Other substrates sold for birdcages include pine shavings, corncob pellets, and recycled newspaper bedding. Your bird may try to eat these items and become ill, perhaps even die from them. Also, these types of bedding don't allow you to see your bird's droppings, which is essential to keeping him healthy. What if there's blood in the droppings, undigested food, or worms? You will see these things on the newspaper but not on the other types of bedding. You also do not need the sandpaper "cutouts" sold for certain styles of cages. These do nothing for your bird—save your money for bird treats instead.

## Seed Catchers

Unless your birds live outside or in an acrylic cage, you're going to need some kind of seed and debris catcher on

You can include rope perches in your canary cage, but you must snip off any frayed bits for your bird's safety.

your cage. Some cages come with these already attached or as an accessory option. For other cages, you'll have to buy them separately. You also can use a thin layer of plastic attached to the bottom half of the cage, or a "birdie bloomer," a kind of fabric shower cap made to slip over the bottom of the cage. In my experience, the cages that come with a seed skirt as part of the cage stay the tidiest.

### Cuttlebone and Mineral Block

The cuttlebone and mineral block could easily be put in the diet and nutrition chapter, but they are sold in the bird accessory aisle in the pet shop, so they're worth mentioning here. The cuttlebone is part of a type of squid that adds calcium to the canary diet; the mineral block also adds calcium, but the amount of calcium is contingent upon how much the canary likes either of these additions to the cage. They also can help to keep the beak trim. Both are inexpensive and easy to get, so it's worth it to include them.

### Cage Cover

If your house isn't drafty and you don't mind hearing bird song in the morning, you don't really need a cage cover. However, if you're a night owl and you want to put your canary to bed at a reasonable hour, you'll need to cover the cage at night and then remember to uncover it in the morning. You can buy a custom-fitted cover for the cage, or you can use a cotton blanket or dark

## Mirror, Mirror

Canaries love toys, especially those with fibers and threads to pluck. Be careful if you offer a mirrored toy—the bird may fall in love with its reflection and stare at himself rather than eat!

sheet. Only cover your canary in the evening. He needs both daytime and nighttime hours.

### Setting Up the Cage

Putting all of your bird's accessories in the cage is easy once you've set up the cage and have placed it where you want it. Here's a quick blueprint:

1. Place food and water cups about a third of the way from the top of the cage. They shouldn't be so low that the bird may soil them, and they shouldn't be so high that they're inaccessible.

2. Place a perch or two just under the food and water dishes. Put a couple of perches below them

but going the opposite way—in other words, two should go front to back, and two or more should go side to side. Don't crowd the cage! The bird should be able to fly without knocking into perches and toys.

3. Place a swing in the center of the cage, but make sure that it doesn't hit anything else when it swings around.

4. Place toys at the sides of the cage so that they are accessible from the perches.

### Other Canary Supplies

Beyond housing and accessories, your canary needs a few more items to round out his supplies.

*Most canaries enjoy swings, so include one in your bird's cage.*

*If you allow your canary out for exercise, be certain that any houseplants you have are nonpoisonous.*

## Cage Cleaning Supplies

Many household cleansers are deadly to your bird, so don't use any chemicals in or around his cage. Instead, use natural disinfectants, such as vinegar for disinfecting and baking soda for scrubbing. You can use a 10 percent bleach solution for soaking components of the cage, but rinse very thoroughly. Grapefruit seed extract also makes a great disinfectant, and you only need 32 drops per quart (liter) and a cheap spray bottle to use it effectively. This extract is safe to ingest and can be used all over the house.

## Grooming Supplies

You're not going to be doing much grooming for your canary, but you will probably need a safe nail clipper. I'll go into more detail on what type is best and how to use it in Chapter 4.

## Lighting

Invest in bird lamps if you live in a part of the country that gets cold and dark for a good portion of the year. You can get special wide-spectrum lightbulbs that mimic the sun's rays.

Buy a standard, cheap spot lamp from the hardware store and shine it a few feet (about a meter) away from your canary's cage. If you can't find bird-specific bulbs, use bulbs made for reptiles. Ideally, the light from the lamp should come from above, so invest in a hanging fluorescent lamp fixture if you can.

Giving your bird the proper amount of light will help to keep his (or her) hormones in check. Too many hours of light and the birds will go into breeding mode; too few hours and they will never

## Cage Mainenance Schedule

Here's a simple cleaning schedule that should help to keep your canary healthy:

*Daily:* Remove and replace the newspaper at the bottom of the cage every day (or every other day).

*Weekly:* Clean perches by washing them in hot soapy water and drying them thoroughly. Clean the bottom grate by scraping it and then washing it in hot soapy water.

*Monthly:* Clean the entire cage, either by dismantling it and hosing it outside or in the tub, or if the cage is large, by using a high-pressure cleaner.

Additionally, clean toys every other week or as necessary.

breed. Ideally, if you're just keeping a companion canary, you'll want to give your bird about 10 to 11 hours of light a day. You'll find more information about breeding canaries in Chapter 6.

## Nesting Materials

If you want to breed your canaries, you'll need some nesting materials. I'll tell you all you need to know about canary breeding and nesting in Chapter 6.

## Travel Carrier

Even if you don't plan to take trips with your canary, you will need a travel carrier in case of emergencies. The carrier should be easy to clean and small enough to fit beneath the seat of an airplane. It also should have adequate ventilation and a place to put food and water dishes. Ideally, a bird carrier opens from both the top and the side, making it easier to catch a squirming bird.

# Chapter 3

# Eating Well

Proper nutrition can make the difference between a healthy, beautiful, singing canary and one who becomes ill, perhaps even dies well before his time. Yes, avian nutrition is that important. No animal can thrive without quality food and proper nutrition.

In the past, bird food was largely designed with convenience in mind, not nutrition and longevity. It was easy to open a bag of seed and just pour it in a dish. Fortunately, bird food manufacturers and avian experts have come a long way in their thinking and research on the topic, and companion birds have reaped the benefits. Sure, seed is still part of the general canary diet, but it's only part of the story when it comes to canary nutrition.

## The Diet of the Wild Canary

The basic diet of the wild canary is seed, but they also eat fruit, other vegetation, and insects. The wild diet is fairly simple, making this a pretty easy bird to feed in captivity.

Your canary needs many of the same nutrients that you need to be healthy. And like you, the bottom line for a canary's nutritional health is variety. The more food items that you feed, the more likely that your bird will eat something healthy. Don't give up on a bird who seems finicky. He will eat what you're offering if you keep offering it. His curiosity will get the best of him. Canaries are more "instinctual" than parrots in some senses. They don't imprint in the same way on human life, so eating doesn't become a battle of wills. They will eat pretty much what you put in front of them if they deem it edible.

## Three Important Nutrients

Here are just three of the many important vitamins and minerals that your canary requires.

### Calcium

Calcium is essential for bones and body function; lack of calcium can cause seizures, and a deficiency also can cause egg binding in hens. For birds, it is available in fortified products, kale, mustard greens and other greens, and almonds. It also can be supplemented in the diet by offering cuttlebone or by putting a calcium supplement into the food or water.

## Feeding Schedule

Feed your canary first thing in the morning with his daily protein source—usually egg food—and his fruits and veggies. Once he's chowing down on these goodies, add his daily ration of seed. If you live in a warm climate, remove all soft foods before they spoil. Also, change the water at least once a day, and always make sure that water dishes are full.

In nature, canaries feed mainly on grass seeds, but also eat other seeds, leaves, fruit, and insects.

## Vitamin A

Vitamin A is the most essential vitamin for birds because it promotes respiratory and liver health. For birds, this vitamin is available in leafy greens and orange vegetables. Do not supplement vitamin A without a veterinarian's supervision because too much can be toxic.

## Vitamin C

Vitamin C is necessary for the immune system. For birds, it is available in kale, red peppers, strawberries, and oranges.

## Birdseed

There has been a lot of debate recently about whether or not birdseed is actually good for birds. Well, for some birds, it is sorely lacking in many vitamins and minerals and doesn't make a good base diet. For the canary, though, seed makes a great base diet because it's the base diet for his wild cousins—this bird is genetically programmed to do well on seed. This isn't to say that all you should offer is seed; that's a deadly diet for any bird. But seed as a base diet is fine, along with a variety of fruits, veggies, and proteins.

Choosing the right kind of seed isn't difficult. You'll likely find a bag of seed with a canary's image printed right on it. Most seed mixes contain primarily millet, with some oat groats, safflower seeds, canary seeds, buckwheat, rapeseed, flaxseed, and others mixed in. If you have a feed store nearby, you can create your own mix with the seeds that your canary likes best so that there's less waste. The all-in-one mixes don't suit every bird.

Here are some of the seeds that canaries particularly like:

- **Canary seed:** Yes, there's a grass seed named after your bird! Canaries relish this small seed, which can compose the majority of the seed mix.
- **Rapeseed:** This is the round seed that makes canola oil. It can compose up to 30 percent of the seed mix.
- **Millet:** Millet is a grain, closely related to wheat, that comes in a variety of subspecies. Most canary mixes will have white millet or proso millet. It contains about 11 percent protein. Millet spray makes a great treat,

especially for weaning birds, ill birds who are having a hard time eating, or those who are a bit fussy about their diet.

Watch to see what your canary is actually eating and what he likes best, and then tailor a seed mix to what he favors most. You can usually buy bulk seeds at bird stores or online. Buying a mix that's packed full of seeds that your canary won't eat is a waste of money.

Some of the seed mixes found in pet stores are brightly colored and claim to be "fortified" with vitamins. These vitamins are in the coloring that the manufacturer coats on the outside of the seed. The inside, the only part that your canary actually eats, remains uncoated. Save your money and buy

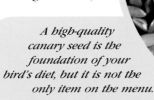

*A high-quality canary seed is the foundation of your bird's diet, but it is not the only item on the menu.*

the plain-looking seed at a feed store, and spend the difference on healthy fruits and vegetables for your bird. The regular seed is not as colorful, but it's less expensive and will suit your bird just fine.

Remember that your canary will only really eat from the top layer of seed, so make sure to clean out the hulls and offer new seed every day, even if it looks like the bowl is full. Many novice birdkeepers have starved their birds to death thinking that the empty seed hulls are just uneaten seeds.

## Sprouting Seeds

Seeds that have been sprouted are much higher in nutrition than dry seeds, so if you have some time, you can make your bird's favorite food into something very healthy that you can serve in large amounts every day. Remember in elementary school when you sprouted dry beans in a jar? Sprouting seeds is that easy. You can buy sprouted beans at the supermarket, or you can sprout seeds and beans on your own using a sprouting kit from any health food store. Some companies sell a sprouting kit for birds that you can use right out of the box.

You don't need a green thumb to follow these simple steps:

1. Rinse the seeds and soak them overnight in cool, clean water.
2. Line the bottom of a shallow, flat

## Water: It's Essential

It's essential that you provide the best water possible for your bird. Canaries have very small bodies, and the buildup of metals and toxins happens much more quickly than in humans, so try not to use water straight from the tap. It contains chlorine, which can leach important nutrients from your bird's body. Bottled drinking water or filtered water is a much better option.

Fresh water should always be available—a canary can die after just a few hours of being denied water.

dish with wet paper towels, and spread the seeds in a single layer on top of them.

3. Cover the dish with plastic wrap and punch several holes in it.
4. Place the pan somewhere warm where it also will receive light.
5. Make sure that the paper towels don't dry out.
6. In three to five days, when the seeds are sufficiently sprouted, rinse them in cold water and store them in the refrigerator.

Sprouted seeds tend to spoil quickly, so keep an eye (and a nose!) on them. Don't offer your canary rancid or moldy seed. If you notice an odor coming from the seeds or they feel sticky, toss them out. A good trick is to put a few drops of grapefruit seed extract into the water of your last rinse. You can find it in any health food store or online. This extract is perfectly safe for use with birds (and humans) and is actually healthful. It has antibacterial, antifungal, and antiviral properties. You can even put a couple of drops of it into your bird's water a few days a week.

Sprouting seeds is also how you can tell good seeds from those that aren't viable anymore—in other words, dead seeds. You should always test a bag of seeds before you offer it to your birds. Just put 1 teaspoon of seeds onto a wet paper towel, put it on the windowsill, and keep it moist. If none of the seeds sprout, you have bought old, dead seeds. If only some sprout, you have a bag that's on the way out. If they all sprout, then you have good seeds and can rely on that source.

A canary will need about 2 tablespoons of seed a day, along with his other foods. However, you should offer more seeds than that in case you forget to feed him one day—a canary may die after just a day of not eating. A canary's metabolism is high, so he cannot be without food for very long.

## Pelleted Foods

Pellets emerged on the avian scene a number of years ago and have become a prominent trend in feeding birds. They are a combination of healthful ingredients, usually seeds and grains, that the manufacturer shapes into bits that resemble seeds and other foods that birds find interesting, kind of like the way dog or cat food is made. There are countless brands on the market, each claiming that their product is the best. Although pellets can contain some good stuff, there has been a backlash recently against feeding them as a total diet. Long-term use of a pellet-only diet has shown results similar to

*Most canaries enjoy millet spray, which makes it a great treat to give to your bird.*

## Children and Canary Feeding

Parents of young children should always supervise a pet's care. Even though a canary might be a child's companion, his nutritional needs are best left to adults. A child may forget to feed a pet, and a canary can die after a couple days of starvation. A child can definitely help, however, by measuring out the bird's seed ration for the day, or if old enough to help in the kitchen, can wash fruits and veggies and offer them to the bird once an adult has chopped them. If your child really wants to help with the bird, make cooking the egg food a fun ritual that your child can help with. Have her crack the eggs and add the ingredients.

long-term use of an all-seed diet.

As with seeds, pellets are not bad, but they are not the only food you should feed your canary. Variety is key. Pellets are a good base diet, but feeding them does not mean that you should exclude other foods, such as fruits and vegetables, table foods, and some seeds. Pellets can compose 40 to 50 percent of your canary's total diet, with the rest consisting of other healthy foods.

Check the label on the pellets you buy. Try only to buy all-natural, preservative-free, organic pellets. You might notice that the seed mix you use has pellets in it. Be aware of what your canary is actually eating. You may be paying for pellets that your bird isn't consuming, which is a waste of money.

The seed-versus-pellet debate continues among bird experts. The seed camp will never touch pellets, and the pellet camp feels that seed is terrible. Then there are some birdkeepers who feed both. Beware of the person who tells you to exclude one over the other. Seeds given in moderation are not going to harm your bird, especially a canary, who

51

## Check the Bowls

Canaries hull their seeds, so even though the food dish may look full, it may just be full of seed shells. Add fresh food to the top of the cup every day. This is important because a canary deprived of food will not live much more than 48 hours. A canary deprived of water will not live much more than 24 hours. Check food and water dishes often!

does very well on seed. But pellets can be a decent base diet if you also offer other foods. Use your own judgment and the advice of your veterinarian. Remember that canaries are seed eaters in the wild, and their bodies are built to metabolize it well.

If you have decided to convert your canary from a seed-based diet to a pellet-based diet, get the go-ahead from your avian veterinarian first. Conversion can be stressful, and your canary should be in prime condition before you make the switch.

After your veterinarian approves the switch, mix the pellets with the seed in a 50/50 ratio so that your canary gets used to seeing the pellets. Gradually reduce the ratio of seeds to pellets each week until you're only feeding pellets by the fifth or sixth week. Keep offering lots of other foods at this time as well, especially healthy fruits, vegetables, a protein source, and cooked foods.

Make sure that your canary is actually eating the pellets before you completely remove seed from his diet. Canaries can starve to death and can otherwise be severely affected by not eating for as little as a day and a half. Never try to convert breeding birds or sick birds, and never make your canary switch cold turkey. Younger canaries will have an easier time converting than older canaries, so

start early. Some pet stores or breeders wean their birds onto pellets, so be sure to ask about the bird's diet before you bring him home. It's likely that your canary has been weaned onto seed.

## Fruits and Vegetables

Fruits and vegetables contain vitamins and minerals that are important to your canary's diet—and they make a fun addition to it as well. Most canaries don't have a lot to do all day, so playing with different kinds of

*Feed your canaries every day, preferably in the morning.*

## Pesticides

It's important to remember to thoroughly rinse all produce before offering it to your bird. His body is small, so the slightest traces of pesticides could endanger him. Feed organic fruits and veggies if you can.

foods offers a great distraction. Try to feed at least four to six fresh vegetables and fruits a day—more if you can—especially well-washed leafy greens. Eventually, you'll get to know what your canary's favorites are, and you can keep them on hand.

The best fruits and vegetables for your bird are deep green or orange in color. This type of produce has the most nutrients, especially vitamin A, which your canary needs to maintain a healthy respiratory system. Vitamin A-deficient birds are prone to respiratory, skin, and liver problems.

Wash all fruits and vegetables thoroughly before serving them to your canary. His body is small and can be affected by even the tiniest traces of pesticides. Offer organic produce if you can so that you have one less thing to worry about.

*Many garden plants, including mints, are safe treats for canaries, provided you don't spray them with pesticides or other chemicals.*

Fruits and vegetables sour quickly in warm weather, so remove them a few hours after you offer them and replace them with a new batch at this time if that's convenient. Leave these foods with the bird longer in cooler weather, but make sure to remove them in the evening.

Try chopping, grating, slicing, or offering the food whole. Clipping greens to the side of the cage is a

great way to get your canary interested in them. Be patient. Offer new things week after week. Canaries are curious by nature and will eventually try the new food. Offer a dish of shredded beets and carrots, or try serving various types of greens in shallow dishes full of water. Some birds will bathe in the greens and then dine on them. Each bird's preferences are different.

If your canary is still fussy after a few weeks, perhaps it's because he's afraid of the dish you're using, or he's not happy with the way you're offering the food. Perhaps the food is too big or too small. Change the dishes. Cook the

*You will need to feed a color-enhancing diet to Red Factor canaries if you want to maintain their bright plumage.*

vegetables. You can even bake or cook fresh veggies and fruits into breads, casseroles, and other meals. If you're pressed for time, use frozen vegetables and fruits. They aren't as good as using fresh produce, but if that's all you have time for on a particular day, they are better than nothing. Never use canned veggies, however, because they contain too much salt. Also, limit citrus to one day a week—it may interfere with your canary's ability to absorb needed iron.

## Cooked Diet

Another good addition to your base diet is a cooked diet, which you can buy commercially or make on your own. These diets contain grains, dehydrated veggies and fruits, and supplements. They are easy to cook and keep in the refrigerator for a week.

If you want to make a cooked diet yourself, soak and cook a few types of beans (kidney, lentil, white, garbanzo, etc.), make three or four types of healthy grains (brown rice, amaranth, barley, red wheat, whole oats, etc.), make a batch of couscous, and lightly sauté some veggies (kale, carrots, yams, tomato, parsley, etc.) in olive or canola oil. Mix everything together, and freeze in small, clear plastic bags for your daily portions. Thaw before serving. If you're using the microwave to thaw

# Supplements

You may have seen water vitamin or mineral supplements in the bird section of your local pet shop. These companion-grade supplements will probably not harm your bird, but shouldn't be necessary if you provide a healthy, balanced diet. Before you consider offering them, try to get your canary to eat fruits and vegetables that are rich in vitamins, especially vitamin A. These include carrots, sweet potatoes, kale, spinach, butternut squash, mangoes, red peppers, and turnip greens.

You can supplement moist food by sprinkling spirulina or green food powder over it. Probiotics, like acidophilus, help to balance a bird's digestive and immune systems and can be offered in the water a few days a week or sprinkled over moist foods. If you do decide to add vitamins to your canary's water, be sure that you change it frequently. Most veterinarians are opposed to water supplements for birds, but many keepers find a good-quality supplement useful a couple of days a week. Many keepers also add one or two drops of apple cider vinegar to their water daily; the acidity in it wards off bacteria and is healthful for your bird. Finally, a couple of drops of grapefruit seed extract in the water a few days a week helps to ward off viruses, fungi, and bacteria.

## Insects

It's not typical to feed canaries insects, but they will eat them if offered. Try very small mealworms, wax worms, or soft grubs. You can often find live worms at pet stores, but you also can order them online. Mealworms are extremely easy to propagate, too, if you have the patience and the stomach for it. (I used to do it, and it was kind of fun!) If your canary doesn't eat the worms you offer, don't press the issue. They're a good source of protein but not necessary.

## Table Foods

Healthy table foods can be a great addition to your canary's diet. With very few exceptions, your bird can eat anything and everything that you eat. Don't worry about spices; birds can eat the hottest of peppers because they have fewer taste receptors on their tongues. A good rule for table foods for birds is that if it's good for you, it's probably good for the bird, and if it's bad for you, it's probably bad for the bird. So although junk food is tasty, the salt and fat can be deadly to your little canary. Also never give any bird avocado, chocolate, alcohol, or caffeine, which are all toxic to birds.

Eggs offer a lot of nutrients, and canaries usually love them. Boil eggs for about 30 minutes, cool them, and then crush them, shell and all. Make sure to boil the eggs well because those eggs came from a chicken that could

## Toxic Foods

Although birds can basically eat what we eat, be aware that some foods are toxic to them and can be fatal:

- alcohol
- avocado
- caffeine
- carbonated beverages
- chocolate
- dried beans
- mushrooms
- pits and fruit seeds
- raw onions
- salty/sugary/fatty foods

the portions, make sure that there are no hot spots in the food before you serve it. To get your canary used to eating a cooked diet, sprinkle his favorite seeds over the mixture to attract him to the bowl.

If you enjoy baking, you also can make "birdie bread" simply by adding healthy veggies, pellets, nuts, and other items to commercially prepared corn muffin mix. Only feed this to healthy birds who have no history of yeast infections. This is more of a treat than a base diet, but you can offer it a couple of times a week and it freezes well.

*Canaries will enjoy table foods along with seeds and pellets.*

potentially pass a disease on to your canary. If you're a whiz in the kitchen (or even if you're not), you can scramble eggs with some pellets or fresh chopped veggies. Add some grated soy cheese for some extra protein. (A bird's digestion isn't really set up to handle cheese or any dairy products.)

Whole-wheat and nutty grain breads are great additions to the diet. Whole-wheat crackers are good, too, but be sure that they're unsalted. Whole-wheat pasta in various shapes makes a nice meal, especially if you add grated veggies and other grains.

Birds can even eat well-cooked flesh meats, like chicken and fish, but in moderation. Offer these no more than one time a week.

## Protein

Protein is really important to the canary diet, so a quality protein source should be offered every day. One of the best sources of protein that your canary will really like is "egg food." You can purchase a

## Canaries and Eggs

It might seem cannibalistic, but eggs are very healthy for canaries. In fact, you can serve them the whole egg, shell and all. Make sure to boil eggs very well for at least 30 to 40 minutes; this will kill bacteria and other germs that can infect your bird. After the eggs are boiled, mash them well and serve. You can even mash them with wheat germ and spirulina. Or, if you feel like cooking, make very dry scrambled eggs, shell and all, and toss in some seed to get the birds interested.

Rather than feeding commercially prepared grit, which can sometimes cause medical problems, use eggshells instead. Save some eggshells from your morning breakfast, wash them very well, and then bake them for 45 minutes on 300°F (149°C). Cool them well, and then crunch them up. Serve in a shallow dish or sprinkle over regular food. Eggshells provide a much-needed source of calcium.

commercially prepared egg food, but it's easy and fun to make yourself. You can even blend the two for a protein-packed punch. Here's an easy recipe:

- Scramble five eggs, shells and all, and cook them well.
- Mash the scrambled eggs up well—an electronic mixer is good for this. Make sure that the shells become very small pieces.
- Add a couple of teaspoons of an avian vitamin supplement and a powdered mineral supplement.
- Add 2 tablespoons of wheat germ oil.
- Mix in 2 cups (0.5 l) (give or take) of commercially prepared egg food. This recipe freezes well. Place

servings in small, clear plastic bags, and thaw one each day for your bird to eat.

## Color Feeding

Some color-bred canaries, like the Red Factor, are color fed, meaning that they must be fed specific foods and chemicals so that they retain their bright orange or red colors. Color feeding can be tricky—not enough and the bird will molt out too light in color, but too much and the bird can develop serious health issues.

Color-bred canaries get their color from canthaxanthin, beta-carotene, or orange carotenoids, usually a combination of two or more of these. You can purchase these chemicals premixed, ready to go into the bird's water. Follow the directions on the package, and don't offer more than suggested—more is not better. As a little side note, canthaxanthin is an ingredient in human tanning pills, but it has been reported that the chemical may cause liver and eye damage in humans.

Color-bred canaries will also take color from natural sources, like carrots, paprika, beets, yams, tomatoes, cherries, and orange squash. You can feed your bird as much of these natural sources of color as you'd like.

## The Expert Knows

### Grit for Digestion?

Grit is a popularly sold dietary supplement available in any pet store. There are two types: soluble, like oyster shells and cuttlebone, and insoluble, like silica. It is a common myth that parrots need grit in their diet, but they don't. Canaries, however, can benefit from a small amount of grit. Some evidence shows that small amounts of grit can aid digestion. Freely feeding grit is not recommended, however, because too much can cause a blocked up the crop (crop impaction), which can be fatal. Offering small amounts of soluble grit once a week in a separate cup is acceptable.

# Fresh Veggies and Fruits

Here's a short list of fruits and veggies that are good to offer your canary.

**Vegetables:**
beans (cooked)
beets
bell peppers
broccoli
cabbage
carrots
cauliflower
celery
cilantro
corn
cucumbers
endive
green beans
greens (all kinds)
hot peppers

peas
potatoes (cooked)
pumpkin
radicchio
spinach
sprouts
squash (any kind)
sweet potatoes
tomatoes
turnips
watercress
yams
zucchini

**Fruits:**
apples

cactus fruit
cantaloupe
dates
figs
grapes
honeydew
kiwis
mangoes
oranges
papayas
passion fruit
peaches
pears
pineapples
plums
pomegranates

# Chapter 4

# Looking Good

Some canaries are beautiful and vividly bright; others are fluffy or crested; still others would blend right in with the woodwork. Whatever the case, canaries take a lot of pride in their appearance. They primp and preen and bathe constantly, but they aren't being vain—they're just doing what birds do to maintain their health and their ability to fly and keep warm.

F eathers are a real miracle of nature: They keep a bird warm and cool as needed, they repel water, and they are strong enough to enable flight. No wonder the canary wants to take care of them! This chapter will show you how to help your canary stay clean and looking great.

## The Wonder of Feathers

A single feather is a fairly delicate object, but when feathers are layered on a bird, they offer protection from the weather, a heating and cooling system, and of course, flight. Feathers are made of keratin, the same material as human hair and nails. The feather starts at the follicle, which extends outward into a shaft, called the calamus. Once the calamus extends beyond the follicle, it is called the rachis. (That's the line in the middle of the feather.) Barbs grow on either side of the rachis, and on the barbs (in larger feathers, like the flight feathers) grow barbules. On each of the barbules are hooklets, which behave kind of like

Velcro, hooking the barbules together. The barbules do come apart, but the bird can zip them up again during preening. Feathers that have barbules hooked together are called pennaceous, and feathers that don't have them hooked together (like down feathers near the skin) are called plumaceous. It all sounds really complicated, but fortunately, the birds know exactly how to grow them!

## Preening

Preening is the act of cleaning and organizing the feathers. People new to birds often wonder if a bird is itchy or picking at parasites when he's preening. No, he's just giving each feather a once-over to make sure that it's neat and clean. Feathers are actually made of various strands that "zip" together kind of like a zipper. Even though the components of feathers seem very delicate, when they're all zipped up working together with other feathers, they're actually incredibly strong. So when you see a bird preening, part of what he's doing is zipping the feather components together to make sure that each feather has integrity.

Paired birds will often preen each other. This is called allopreening and

*Canaries spend much of their time preening. In nature, survival depends on good feather condition.*

## Baldness

Although bald patches in a canary can often indicate illness or stress, baldness also can be congenital, the result of a pairing of two canaries who have the crested gene. There are some other mutations that cause head baldness when bred together as well.

Baldness also can happen when a canary doesn't have enough protein or nutrition during a molt. If you see baldness in one of your canaries, also consider territorial disputes—it's possible that one of the canaries is plucking the others.

is a form of bonding. Birds can't reach some places on their bodies, like the top of the head, so it's nice to have a mate who can reach for them.

## Molting

Molting is a bird's way of replacing feathers that are worn out. The bird will systematically lose feathers from all over his body but not all at once and not in patches—bald patches can be a sign of illness or stress in a canary. You will notice more feathers on the bottom of the cage than usual and will see pinfeathers emerging from between the other feathers. Molts occur once or twice a year and can last a few months, although canaries can go through a "soft molt," where they lose and grow feathers all year long.

Generally, canaries will not sing during a molt (although some do), so don't become concerned if Tweety stops his usual concerto during molting time. Offer your bird a nutritious diet at this time to help with

*Give your canary the opportunity to bathe every day—it's good for his feathers and fun for him, too.*

feather production, and include some extra protein. Also, get a CD of canary songs, and play it during a molt when your singer is taking a break. He may actually learn something new.

## Bathing

Bathing is as important to canaries as it is to humans, perhaps even more

### Diet for Good Feathers

Molting birds (and those who are feeding and weaning babies) need more nutrition to maintain their weight, health, and feather quality. In particular, offer egg food, either a commercial variety or one that you make at home. (See the recipe for homemade egg food in Chapter 3.) Also offer green foods, such as well-washed collards, romaine, spinach, kale, or watercress. Cucumber is also a relished treat, but try to offer only organic. Commercially prepared canary biscuits are good, too, as are parrot biscuits (used to be called "monkey chow") soaked in water or apple juice; remove them after a few hours because they spoil easily.

so. The feathers have to be clean and free of debris for a bird to fly. Fortunately, canaries have the instinct and urge to bathe themselves—they don't need a scheduled "bath time." You don't have to do anything more than offer your canary a shallow dish of tepid water every day. Most canaries also will bathe in their regular water dish, which is why you should clean the water a couple of times a day, at least.

Another fun way to get your canary to bathe is to offer a dish full of wet greens, like spinach, baby lettuce, or kale. Just wash the greens well and put them in a shallow dish of water. Your bird may jump right into the greens and go to town, crouching down and fluttering in the damp veggies. He may want to munch on them, too, which is quite healthy.

Some canaries will appreciate a misting shower, although others won't like this at all. If you want to try it, get a mister that sprays very fine water droplets and spray it on your canary while he's bathing. He may appreciate the extra help and feel like he's enjoying a natural rain shower. On the other hand, he may not like it at all. If he doesn't appreciate it, don't push the issue. Also, a mister will dampen the cage, so remove all food and paper before you mist and be sure to dry the cage after the bath.

## Kids and Bath Time

Not a lot of kids like bath time, but canaries love it. There isn't much grooming needed with canaries, but offering a bath is really simple and very healthy for your bird. Let your child fill a shallow dish with tepid water and place it gently in the cage. Once the canary is done, let your child remove the dish and change the damp paper at the bottom of the cage. She might learn that bath time isn't so bad after all!

## Nail Care

For the most part, you will not have to trim your canary's nails if you provide him with rough landing surfaces, like concrete and sand perches (but not sandpaper perch sheaths). However, some canaries' nails do grow pretty long, so you'll have to intervene and trim the nails. The nails should be the shape of a gentle half-moon. If they are longer, perhaps even forming spirals, your canary will have a difficult time perching and could eventually have foot and leg problems—and even lameness.

If you're unsure about clipping the nails or you're a little squeamish about it, have your local avian veterinarian or bird shop groomer trim the nails for you. If you want to do it yourself, you have to consider two things. First, you have to hold your bird safely and properly, and secondly, you have to trim the nails correctly.

To hold a canary, grasp him in one hand with his back in your palm and his head between your first and second fingers. You'll be placing more pressure on his neck than around his chest. If you restrict his chest, he will not be able to breathe at all.

If you're new at this, nail trimming is best done as a two-person job. One person holds the bird while the other carefully trims the toenails. Like our nails, if they are cut too short, the nail will bleed. The blood supply in the nail is called the "quick" and can be seen easily in light-colored nails as a red line. You want to cut up to the red line but not beyond it. The quick is tougher to see with dark nails, but if you trim the nails near a lightbulb, you may be able to see through them. If not, do a very conservative clip. Ideally, the entire procedure should only take you a minute or two.

If you do happen to cut into the quick and your canary bleeds, you will need some styptic powder on hand to stop the bleeding. You can get it at just about any pet shop. (Only use styptic powder on nails, not on any other bleeding areas.) If you don't have styptic powder in the house, you

65

activities with his beak that will naturally wear it down, such as eating hard foods, playing with toys, and wiping it on perches. If your canary's beak seems overgrown, he may have a health disorder that needs to be addressed by a veterinarian.

Scaly face mites, or *Knemidocoptes* or *Cnemidocoptes*, can infect the beak (and legs), causing it to overgrow or become misshapen. The legs and the cere (where the nostrils are located) can be infected with lesions. Mites are then transmitted from parents to chicks and live their whole life cycle on the bird. They can be transmitted from bird to bird with close contact. Treatment by a veterinarian is easy and effective. Mite protectors are ineffective for preventing these pests.

Malnutrition also can cause the beak to overgrow, so if you notice any deformation or abnormality with the beak, seek medical advice. *Never* trim your bird's beak because you can severely injure him if you don't know what you're doing. A canary may not recover from even the slightest slip. It

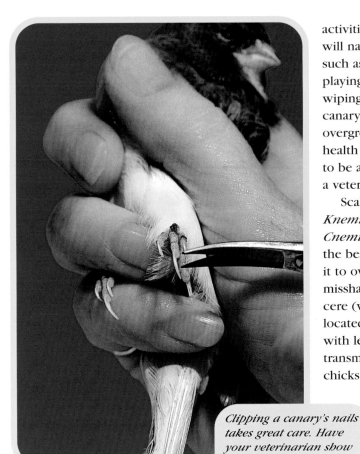

*Clipping a canary's nails takes great care. Have your veterinarian show you how before you attempt it on your own.*

can use flour or cornstarch to stop the bleeding. Just press a little bit into the bleeding nail and apply gentle pressure for a few seconds.

## Beak Care

The canary's beak is made of the same protein material as his nails (and our nails), keratin, and is built over a honeycomb-like structure that makes it very light. A healthy bird does cannot be stressed enough—if you notice something wrong with your bird's beak, make an appointment with your avian veterinarian.

Sometimes the beak isn't aligned properly and becomes "scissored" rather than coming together like a clamshell. This beak does need to be trimmed or filed every so often to allow it to start to grow regularly. Your veterinarian or a bird expert is the only person who should perform this procedure.

## Wing Clipping

Unlike some parrots, a canary's wings are not typically clipped. Because these birds are generally "watching only" companions, there is no need to clip the wings. Even if you want to try to tame your canary, do not clip his wings. Taming a canary is less about forcing

## Grooming Supplies

Grooming supplies for a canary are simple. You only need two items:
- A shallow dish to act as a birdbath. An inch (2.5 cm) of plain room temperature water is fine. You don't need any fancy store-bought birdbath sprays. These can actually be irritating to a canary.
- A pair of sharp notched nail clippers made for cutting tiny nails.

him to sit on your finger and more about taking the time to lure him to you with food and having him start to trust you gradually. If you clip your bird's wings, you may just scare him to death. Don't do it!

# Chapter 5

# Feeling Good

Although canaries are tiny birds and health care might seem straightforward or even unnecessary, they are actually quite complex and need good preventive veterinary care, as well as care when they are ill or have had an injury. Good guardians keep an observant eye on their canaries' daily routine and condition and seek professional care when necessary.

## Finding an Avian Veterinarian

An avian veterinarian specializes in the care and treatment of birds. Birds are obviously quite different from dogs and cats and need a doctor trained in the particular treatment of bird accidents, ailments, and diseases. A veterinarian who does not specialize in birds may not catch a subtle symptom or may not perform the proper tests.

Most people will take a new bird to an avian veterinarian within three days of buying him. There are several good reasons for the visit:

- If you bought your canary with a health guarantee from a shop, you will have some recourse if tests reveal that your new bird is ill.
- You will begin a relationship with the avian veterinarian who will get to know your bird and who will be able to evaluate him better because she will have a "healthy reference" for him.
- Some avian veterinarians will not take an emergency patient unless the bird is a regular client.
- Avian veterinarians often board birds in their offices, although some will only board clients.
- You will receive important recommendations from the vet, including diet and housing advice.
- Canaries can carry zoonotic diseases (those that are transmittable to humans), so it's important to get a

Canaries

## Finding an Avian Veterinarian

Look for the following qualities in a good avian veterinarian:

- Specialty in avian medicine: A vet who's going to treat your birds should specialize in birds only, or birds and other exotics. Board certification is available for avian vets, but it's not necessary.
- Canary care: Ask the doctor if she regularly treats canaries and if she is well versed in canary illnesses and problems.
- Bedside (or cageside) manner: Is the veterinarian friendly and willing to answer questions? You should have enough time with the doctor during the visit to express your concerns and ask pertinent questions.
- Cleanliness: The office should be clean and smell fresh.
- Friendly staff: The office personnel should be friendly and willing to answer questions.
- Quarantine: If your bird has to spend the night, is there a place where he will be quarantined from other sick birds? Ideally, ill birds should be in another structure or a space that has a separate ventilation system.

clean bill of heath before bringing the bird into a home with an infant, elderly person, or someone with a compromised immune system.

*Next to you, your canary's best friend is his avian veterinarian.*

A good place to find an avian veterinarian is by calling the Association of Avian Veterinarians (AAV) at (561) 393-8901 or by looking them up on the Internet at www.aav.org. You also can ask the members of your local bird club or canary society about the doctors they use. Not all veterinarians who treat birds are board certified to do so, although they might be incredibly experienced and adept at bird care.

## The Veterinary Visit

After the initial visit, you should take your canary to the veterinarian for a yearly "well bird" checkup. Some people do this every six months, which isn't a bad idea. The money that you spend on these health checks will be far less than you have to spend on an emergency visit if you notice that your bird is ill. You should definitely schedule these visits if you regularly purchase new birds or if you bird-sit other people's feathered friends. The more birds who come and go from your home, the more risk for illness.

The veterinarian will give your bird a physical examination and weigh him. She may then take cultures from the bird's vent or mouth and take blood for testing. All of these tests show whether or not the bird is in good health, and they are absolutely necessary. Ask your vet which tests are being run and what they will indicate so that you can stay informed.

Most people don't take their canaries in for much, if any, veterinary care, which is a shame. Start your bird off right with a checkup from a qualified avian veterinarian.

## FAMILY-FRIENDLY TIP

### Preparing for the Vet Visit

Going to the doctor isn't fun for anyone, and a child may become concerned about what the veterinarian is going to do with her canary. Explain that the visit is necessary to keep the bird happy and healthy. At most veterinary visits, the doctor will come into the office to speak with you and your child but then take the bird into the back to conduct the testing. Prepare the child for this, and let her know that the bird will come back. Bring some millet spray as a treat that the child can give the bird when the visit is over.

## The Travel Carrier

If you have to take your canary to the groomer or the veterinarian, you'll want to have the right kind of carrier and setup inside the carrier. A small bird carrier, whether plastic or plastic/metal, usually has a small opening at the top so that you can put just your hand through without letting the bird out. Dog and cat carriers typically open at the front, which is too large an opening for a small bird. He will slip right by your arm and fly away!

Line the inside of the carrier with several layers of paper towels, and put some millet spray on top of that. If you're going for just a short distance, there's no need to add water to the carrier. If you're going to be gone more than a couple of hours, or if you're going to be traveling in the heat, add a water bottle or shallow bowl of water to the carrier. (The bowl must be heavily weighted at the bottom to avoid sloshing.) Don't put any perches or toys into the carrier; if you stop short or have an accident, these items may injure your bird. Also, never leave your bird in the car on a very hot or very cold day. Canaries are easily overcome by extreme temperatures.

## General Signs of Illness

A healthy canary is usually active and vocal (during most of the year, but not while molting), and he keeps his feathers in good condition. An ill canary may not keep up with grooming and may "let himself go." He also may look sleepy and listless and spend a lot of time on the bottom of the cage. If you notice anything unusual over an extended period, seek veterinary attention promptly because a bird's condition can decline rapidly.

The first clue that most people get when their bird is ill is a change in attitude, behavior, or routine. There may be changes in the bird's vocalizations, where he stands in the cage, how much he sleeps, the quality of his plumage, and the quality of his breathing. Canaries, like most birds, appreciate routine, and a sudden break in it signals that you should at least investigate his condition. Perhaps something has frightened him or the temperature has dropped or risen too drastically. There are possibilities other than illness. If you can't find any reason for your bird's unusual behavior, look for the following:

- **Attitude change:** Your canary might be ill if he seems listless and is not behaving in his usual manner.
- **Discharge:** If you notice any runniness or discharge from the eyes, nostrils, or vent, take your bird to the veterinarian immediately.
- **Drastic change in droppings:** Your canary's droppings should consist of

## Signs That Your Bird Needs Emergency Care

Any of these conditions require an emergency trip to the veterinarian:

- broken bones
- eye injuries
- gasping for air
- head trauma
- lameness
- loss of consciousness
- loss of limbs
- seizures
- severe bleeding
- vomiting

*You will need some type of travel carrier or travel cage for your canary's trips to the vet.*

## Stress

Just like humans, birds can suffer from stress, and in a canary, stress can be deadly. Canaries who are too confined or who are repeatedly exposed to stressors can become ill. For example, a canary in a tiny cage that's placed in a drafty area will become quite unhappy. Although healthy canaries are active birds, they also can become overweight if they don't get enough exercise. Provide spacious living quarters so that your bird can fly—that's the best exercise for him. The more exercise your canary gets, the healthier, happier, and less stressed he will be.

a solid green portion, white urates (on top of the green), and a clear liquid. If any of these are discolored (darker green, black, yellow, or red) and there has been no change in diet, or if you notice undigested food in the droppings, there might be an illness present. Just remember that some foods (for example, beets and carrots) can change the color of the droppings.

- **Fluffiness:** If you notice that your canary has his feathers fluffed, he is trying to keep heat close to his skin and is having trouble regulating his temperature. Remember, however, that some canaries are supposed to be fluffy, such as the frilled breeds.
- **Food stuck to the feathers around the face:** This indicates poor grooming or vomiting, both possible signs of illness.
- **Lameness:** If your bird can't use his feet, you can be sure that there is a problem. Lameness can occur as a result of egg binding, injury, seizure, or other conditions.
- **Loss of appetite:** You should know how much and what your canary is consuming each day. If you notice that he is not eating enough or that he has stopped eating, there is a problem.
- **Panting or labored breathing:** Either of these symptoms can indicate a respiratory ailment or perhaps overheating.
- **Sleeping too much:** A sick canary may sleep more than usual. Sleeping on the bottom of the cage is especially telling, as is sleeping on two feet instead of one.
- **Tail bobbing:** If the tail is bobbing (front and back) a lot when the bird is breathing, it can indicate a respiratory problem—this bird is laboring to breathe. However, the tail does bob after exercise and while singing, which is normal.

## Signs and Symptoms of Illness

Here are some more points to look for in both a healthy and an ill bird.

### Eyes

A bird can see almost 360 degrees around his environment, which helps him watch for predators and other dangers. Birds also have a second eyelid that acts as a kind of squeegee for the eye, keeping it moist and clean. A healthy eye is clear, moist, and free of discharge. A canary with an eye problem may squint or scratch it excessively with his foot or will rub it on the perch or sides of the cage. Look for swollen eyelids, cloudy eyes, excessive blinking or discharge, and tearing.

*Being housed with a bullying canary will cause the other bird stress. House each canary in his or her own cage to avoid this problem.*

*Feeling Good*

### Ears

Your canary's ears, which are covered by small feathers, are located a short distance parallel to and behind the eyes. You may get a glimpse of an ear after your canary bathes, when the feathers around the head are wet and stuck together.

Birds can't hear in the same range that we do, but they can hear in greater detail. If you can see your canary's ear opening without the bird being wet, make an appointment with your avian veterinarian, or watch carefully to make sure that one canary in the cage isn't plucking the other birds.

*One sign that your canary may be ill is keeping his feathers fluffed up for long periods of time.*

### Beak

Your canary experiences much of his world through his beak. The beak, which is made of the same durable material as our fingernails, grows over a honeycomb-like structure that is basically hollow, a convenient design for an animal that needs to fly. The beak should be aligned, clean, and of a normal length.

### Feet

Birds use their feet to regulate body temperature. During cold weather, they can decrease the amount of blood circulating to their legs and will often draw one leg up into the body and stand only on the other. When canaries are warm, they will increase the blood flow to their legs to cool off. Canaries have little footpads on the bottom of the feet that can become raw or irritated if perching material is too rough. Always offer a variety of perches in a variety of materials.

### Feathers

Feathers are one of the most amazing functional parts of a bird, helping him fly, regulate temperature, and repel water. A healthy canary should be obsessed with taking care of his feathers, preening them for much of the day.

*A healthy canary's eyes will be open, bright, and free of discharge.*

Birds molt about once or twice a year, usually during seasonal changes when periods of sunlight become shorter or longer. Molting is the process by which a bird loses some of the old feathers on his body and grows new ones. When your canary molts, you will notice feathers on the bottom of the cage, but you should not be able to see patches of skin on his body. Male canaries will often stop singing during a molt, which alarms owners but is actually quite normal. Molting birds also might scratch themselves more often as the new feathers break out of their skin. A molting bird will appreciate a daily bath or spraying offered daily, perhaps with a few drops of aloe vera juice mixed in with his water. Molting birds also need a diet richer in protein; the addition of egg food is helpful.

Sometimes a wing or tail feather will break in the middle of the growth process and begin to bleed. This is not a serious injury, and you can deal with it yourself. Keep some styptic powder or cornstarch on hand in case of a bleeding emergency such as this, and apply the product until the bleeding has stopped. Next, you will need to remove the feather with a pair of needle-nosed pliers. While restraining your bird, gently grasp the broken feather with the pliers, close to the shaft, and pull straight out. This will stop the bleeding and prevent infection. If you are too squeamish to do this yourself, take your canary to your avian

## First Aid

Here is a list of essential items for an avian first-aid kit. Keep these items in a small tackle box for convenient access when you need them:

- antibiotic ointment (for small wounds, use a nongreasy product only because oil prevents a bird from retaining body heat)
- alcohol (for sterilizing tools)
- baby bird formula (can be used for adults having a difficult time eating)
- bag or can of your bird's base diet (in case of evacuation)
- bandages and gauze
- bottled water (you may need clean fresh water to flush out a wound or clean your bird of debris)
- cornstarch (to stop bleeding on the skin or beak)
- cotton balls
- cotton swabs (for applying ointment or blotting an area)
- dishwashing detergent (mild, for cleaning oil off feathers)
- electrolyte solution for human babies (for reviving a weak bird)
- eyewash
- heating pad (always allow your bird the option of moving off of the heating pad)
- hydrogen peroxide (always use in a weak solution with water)
- nail clippers
- nail file
- needle-nosed pliers (for broken blood feathers)
- nongreasy first-aid lotion
- penlight
- saline solution
- sanitary wipes
- sharp scissors
- small transport cage
- small clean towels (for holding your bird or swabbing an injury)
- spray bottle (for misting)
- styptic powder (to stop bleeding on the nails)
- tweezers
- veterinarian's telephone number and info

Feeling Good

veterinarian. Usually, even if you don't remove the broken feather, it will work its way out eventually and the bird will be fine.

## Respiratory System

Your canary has a sensitive respiratory system that is susceptible to airborne irritants, such as aerosol sprays, fumes from heated nonstick cookware, and tobacco smoke. Birds don't breathe in the same way humans do. We inhale and exhale, completing one breath. Birds have to take two breaths. The first breath fills the air sacs, located in hollow spaces in the body and in some of the bones, and the second breath pushes the air into the lungs. Remember that coal miners used to take canaries into the mines with them as fume detectors. When the canary dropped dead, they knew it was time to leave the mine.

Birds are prone to respiratory illness and distress because their system is more complicated than ours. If you notice your canary panting

or hear a clicking sound coming from his mouth as he breathes, call your avian veterinarian. Also, always be sure to keep him away from fumes and airborne toxins.

You can recognize a respiratory infection by a change in breathing, tail bobbing (when not singing or panting due to exercise), and even bubbling from the mouth or nostrils. If you notice these symptoms, take your canary to the veterinarian right away.

## Musculoskeletal System

Birds are fantastic athletes, able to fly for miles (kilometers) a day, and as a

*Molting canaries need a diet rich in protein. Most canaries molt once or twice yearly.*

## Dangers of Nonstick Cookware

Nonstick cookware emits toxic fumes when heated, and these fumes are deadly to birds. Birds don't even have to be in the kitchen for the toxicity to overtake them— they can be anywhere in the home. There is no warning sign that birds are about to be overcome; they just drop off their perches, dead. Just before this occurs, they may wheeze and gasp, but by then it's too late to save them. Small birds like canaries are especially susceptible. Avoid nonstick pots and pans, drip plates, burner drip pans, cookie sheets, hair irons, and space heaters, just to name a few common household items.

result, tend to be well muscled. They have more "red" than "white" muscles because they are active flying birds as opposed to grounded birds, such as chickens and turkeys, who don't need as many fat-burning muscles. Many of your canary's bones are filled with air, and all

of them are thin walled, which makes the bird light, a necessary development for flight. A heavy bird would expend a lot more energy in the air.

Although bird bones are strong enough to allow the movement of wings in flight, they are easily broken. If you suspect that one of your canary's bones is broken, take him to the veterinarian immediately. Some of the bones contain air sacs that aid in breathing.

### Digestive System

The canary's digestive system begins with the beak and ends with the vent. After food is swallowed, it goes to the crop, which is near the bird's breast. After going to the crop, the food then goes to the stomach (proventriculus), then on to the gizzard (ventriculus), which grinds the food, and then on to the cloaca, the place where feces and urates collect before being eliminated through the vent. Feces should be semi-solid, green with a white part on top, and have a little moisture around them. You can get a good look at your bird's feces by putting wax paper at the bottom of the cage for a few hours. If you notice any discoloration (that's not because of the food you're feeding), very wet feces, or undigested food in the waste, seek medical attention for your bird.

### Common Illnesses

Now that you know a little bit about the canary's body, here are a few

Older canaries may be less active and prefer to sleep on the bottom of the cage rather than on perches.

diagnose aspergillosis, but it's difficult to treat and may take months of medication and treatment to cure. Prevent this infection by keeping your canary's environment clean and dry, which will prevent the growth of mold.

## Bumblefoot

Bumblefoot is an infection of the bottom of the feet and is associated with poor nutrition, lack of activity, and obesity. The skin on the bottom of the foot may be inflamed and red and may become scabby, resulting in lameness. Use perches with an uneven and bumpy texture, and disinfect perches regularly to avoid this condition.

## Coccidia

Coccidiosis is caused by a parasite, usually affecting birds who are kept outdoors. Testing

diseases and conditions common to this species.

## Aspergillosis

Aspergillosis is a fungal infection caused by a type of mold that causes respiratory distress. It can be deadly if not treated promptly. Any changes in your canary's breathing, changes in vocalization, gasping, or wheezing can indicate this infection. Your avian veterinarian can

## Canary Salad

If your canary becomes soaked in oil (perhaps he was loose and jumped into the salad bowl!), he will no longer be able to regulate his body temperature, a condition that can be deadly. Dust the oil-soaked bird with cornstarch or flour, and then gently bathe him in a small tub of warm water and some mild grease-fighting dish soap. Don't scrub him, and don't wet his head. You may have to repeat this process several times. Keep your bird in a warm area until most of the oil is removed and he is dry.

for this parasite is done by examining the feces under a microscope. However, many birds who have this infection are asymptomatic but will develop symptoms when kept in stressful, crowded, or unsanitary conditions. Symptoms include weight loss, diarrhea, loss of appetite, and change in attitude.

## Giardia

*Giardia* is a one-celled protozoan that can affect your canary, but it also can affect other animals in the house, even yourself (although it's unlikely). It is passed by contaminated food or water and affects the digestive tract. You may notice diarrhea, itching, inability to digest foods, weight loss, and other symptoms. Have your veterinarian test for this parasite if you suspect that your canary is ill. Usually, all of the birds in the household who have been exposed to the ill bird will have to be treated.

## Gout

Gout is a painful condition of the legs common in canaries who don't receive proper nutrition. Symptoms include visible swellings on the legs and subsequent lameness. In general, the "remedy" for birds with gout is a substantial boost in nutrition. You may have to try to

get your canary to take a few drops of liquid vitamins and green food using a small syringe. There is some evidence that a low-protein diet during attacks of gout can help.

## Megabacteria

Megabacteria were once thought to be large bacteria found in parts of the canary's digestive system. Recently, research has shown that what was once called "megabacteria" might actually be a fungal infection. This

*Canaries that are kept without the recommended variety of perches often develop foot problems that need veterinary care.*

illness causes extreme weight loss, and diagnosis generally occurs after death. It is not certain whether these bacteria (or fungi) actually cause the condition or whether a weakened system and poor nutrition allow them to thrive.

## Mites

Air sac mites occur commonly in finches and canaries. They infest the airway and cause a clicking sound when the bird breathes, eventually cutting off the air supply. If you suspect mites because your bird is laboring to breathe, breathing with an open beak, or you hear clicking when the bird breathes, do not try to get rid of them yourself. Contact your avian veterinarian.

Scaly-face mites, or *Knemidokoptes*, occur in young canaries and older birds with a compromised immune system. These mites cause a crusty appearance on the bird's face and legs (in canaries, more commonly on the legs and feet) and can result in an overgrown beak. They are easy to treat with a veterinarian's instructions but require multiple treatments. Scaly-face mites are not very contagious, but they can be passed from bird to bird.

Red mites are somewhat common in canaries, especially if the birds are kept outside. These mites feast on your bird's blood and can weaken him substantially. To check for mites, look carefully in every nook and cranny of the cage in the early morning hours. You will see the little mites engorged with blood, giving them their red color. Consult your veterinarian about the treatment of these mites, which usually involves spraying a mite insecticide several times a day.

The tiny feather mite can infest birds who live outdoors in unclean conditions. These mites eat holes in the feathers, causing the bird to have a ratty appearance. Treatment is similar to that of red mites.

## Overheating

Birds can be overcome by heat easily, especially a small bird like the canary. An overheated bird will pant and spread his wings trying to cool himself. If this is unsuccessful and the heat does not abate, the bird may lose consciousness and even die. If you notice that your bird is becoming overheated, remove him immediately to a cooler place and run a fan near his cage. Lightly mist him with cool water, and offer drops of cool water at the side of his beak. Never set a canary out in the sun unless he has a shady spot where he can retreat, and never leave a canary in a closed car on a warm day.

## Polyomavirus
Polyomavirus usually affects young canaries, although adult birds are carriers, transmitting the disease to their young, who die around the time they are ready to leave the nest. It occurs mainly among breeding stock in crowded conditions, although households with many birds are susceptible as well, especially if you are going to add young birds to the household. There is no treatment for polyomavirus, so prevention is essential. Make sure to have your avian veterinarian test all of your canaries for this disease.

## Psittacosis (Parrot Fever)
Psittacosis, also called chlamydiosis and parrot fever, is transmittable to humans and causes respiratory distress symptoms in both humans and birds. Psittacosis (*Chlamydia psittaci*) is transmitted through droppings and infected secretions.

## Poison Control
If your bird comes in contact with poison and you notice evidence of vomiting; paralysis; bleeding from the eyes, nares, mouth, or vent; seizures; or shock, he may have become poisoned. Call the National Animal Poison Control Center's 24-hour poison hotline at (800) 548-2423, (888) 4-ANIHELP, or (900) 680-0000. If you can, try to discover what your bird has ingested or been exposed to so that the hotline can better help you. Have your credit card ready because the hotline does charge a fee.

Some canaries can be carriers of the disease without showing any symptoms. When symptomatic, symptoms include lime green feces, watery droppings, weakness, change in vocalizations, and a fluffed appearance. Ask your veterinarian to test for this disease, especially if there's someone with a weakened immune system, such as an elderly person or an infant, in contact with your canary.

## Psittacine Beak and Feather Disease (PBFD)

PBFD is an incurable contagious (to other birds) disease that involves feather loss and beak lesions in its later stages. Although canaries aren't the most notorious carriers of this disease, they can get it and transmit it. Diagnosis is through blood testing, and euthanasia is generally recommended after confirmation so that the virus isn't spread to other birds in the household. This disease is fatal and extremely contagious. Symptoms include feather loss, abnormal feather growth, and a generally ill condition.

## Reproductive Disorders

An undernourished egg-laying hen, especially one who hasn't received enough calcium in her diet, may have eggs with soft shells that will be difficult to lay, resulting in egg binding. This also can occur when the egg is malformed or if she has a tumor or other disorder of the reproductive system. Symptoms of egg binding include panting and lameness, and the hen may crouch on the bottom of the cage, fluffed up, obviously in distress. Keeping the laying hen fit and nourished will help to prevent this problem. Consult your veterinarian immediately if you suspect egg binding. (There is more information on this condition in Chapter 6.)

*If you decide to take your bird out for some air, you must make sure that he can get out of the sunlight or he could fatally overheat.*

# All About Air Sacs

Like humans, birds have lungs, but theirs function differently from ours. When we take a breath, our diaphragm pulls air down into the lungs, the oxygen is processed in the lung sacs, and then we breathe out. For birds, air is circulated through a more complex respiratory system that includes air sacs in the bones that use pressure to move air in and out. Birds have to take two breaths for every one of our breaths. Put very simply, when birds breathe in the air goes to a set of air sacs and some of the air goes to the lungs. Then the bird breathes out and breathes in again, and more air goes into the air sacs and then to the lungs. For air to travel the entire respiratory system, the bird requires two respirations. Birds don't have a diaphragm helping to move air into the lungs (an internal mechanism); instead, they have a set of muscles in the chest that contracts to help expel used air. Because of this, it's critical that you do not hold a bird tightly around the chest. Birds can be held very safely around the neck or wrapped loosely in a towel. Also, because the air sacs reach into the bird's bones, a bone break is extremely life threatening and requires immediate medical attention. Infections of the respiratory system are also just as deadly. Birds have a much more efficient and sensitive respiratory system than humans, which is why they are far more sensitive to toxins. This is also why they are such wonderful athletes, able to fly tirelessly for miles (kilometers).

Straining to pass the egg, or even the chronic laying of eggs, can cause the cloaca to prolapse. If you notice red organ-like material sticking outside of the vent, take your hen to the veterinarian immediately.

## Tuberculosis

*Mycobacterium avium* is responsible for the tuberculosis (TB) infection in birds and can be transmitted in food, water, or by filthy cages. Avian tuberculosis can be transmitted to humans with compromised immune systems, so the caretaker must be careful to avoid infection. While TB in humans is a respiratory disease, it is primarily a digestive disorder in canaries. Symptoms in birds include weight loss, lameness, and other digestive disturbances.

## Worms

Roundworms and tapeworms can be found in canaries who are kept in outdoor aviaries and who are allowed access to the ground. Symptoms include vomiting, diarrhea, weight loss, and anemia. If your veterinarian finds roundworms in your bird, schedule routine tests and treatments. Eliminating worms can take quite some time.

## Yeast Infections

Yeast infection, or candidiasis, affects the mouth and digestive tract and can involve the respiratory system. Your canary normally has a certain amount of yeast in his body, but when his bodily balance is out of whack, like when it's undernourished or after a treatment of antibiotics, the fungus yeast can grow to excess.

A canary with a yeast infection will have a sticky substance in his mouth and may have white mouth lesions. Regurgitation and digestive problems may occur. Veterinary treatment is

necessary. Even though this condition is not immediately serious, it can cause death if left untreated. Offering your canary foods that are loaded with vitamin A, such as green leafy vegetables and orange fruits and vegetables, can help to prevent yeast infections.

## The Hospital Cage

Having a hospital cage on hand is important in case of emergencies and illness. It's a comfortable, warm, safe place for your canary to calm down and recuperate. Line a 10-gallon (37.9-l) aquarium with paper towels, and place a heating pad on low to medium underneath one-half of the aquarium— your bird must be able to move away from the heat if it gets too warm. Place a mesh cover on it and drape a towel over three-quarters of the tank. Place a *very* shallow dish of water (a weak bird can drown in even 1 inch [2.5 cm]

*Constant stress can cause your canary many health problems. Try to eliminate stressors—like prowling cats—from his environment.*

## Preventing Loss and Finding the Lost Bird

Seasoned birdkeepers always, by habit, shut and lock a birdcage door. It becomes as natural as breathing. But if you're not used to having birds, it's easy to forget that Tweety is out of the cage. Someone in your home (perhaps yourself) may forget to close a window or door, allowing Tweety to slip outside. When birds fly away, they usually stay relatively close to home for the first few minutes to an hour. If something scares them, they can fly away in a burst and get pretty far in a short amount of time.

If your canary flies away, search the trees and power lines around your yard and the surrounding areas. If you see him, keep an eye on him until dusk, when he'll find a place to roost. Ideally, you can climb to where he's sleeping and net him quickly. This is tough with a canary, though, because most of these types of birds aren't used to being handled and won't allow humans to get too close.

If you can't net your bird on that first night, put up flyers around your neighborhood and at local stores, animal shelters, and veterinary offices. Someone may be able to capture your bird and return him to you, especially if you offer a reward.

of water) on one end, as well as some millet spray and seeds or pellets. Do not include toys or perches, but you may include a rolled-up hand towel. Place the cage in a quiet location, and clean the papers once a day or when they become soiled.

### Senior Canary Care

Canaries can live to be between 5 and 20 years old. In general, breeder females live the shortest, males a little longer, and then the exceptionally cared-for pet the longest. Unfortunately, because canaries are relatively inexpensive, they are often not given the proper care, reducing their life span. Hopefully, your pampered bird will live well into his golden years.

A very elderly bird might have trouble getting around and may need his perches lowered and his food served on the floor of his cage. He might want to sleep on paper towels on the bottom of his cage because his feet may ache. Watch his general condition so that you can catch any health problems early.

Feeling Good

# Chapter 6

# Breeding Canaries

Breeding canaries is a popular hobby among fanciers. There are dozens of canary breeds to experiment with and even more colors and feather types. It's dizzying how many mutations you can play with to get the most interesting-looking and beautiful-sounding birds. However, breeding birds shouldn't be taken lightly. It's a big responsibility, and there's a lot that can go wrong.

I f you have a lot of patience and the willingness to learn all you can about the practice, you may want to try to breed your canaries. It's not as easy as boy meets girl and voila: babies. Breeding canaries is surprisingly complex. This chapter will give you an overview of a few of the things you need to know before you begin. As with most endeavors like this one, you learn the most by doing.

## Choosing a Pair

The first things you need for breeding are a male and a female. Because most

*It is difficult to tell male canaries from female canaries. Only males sing, so that is often the best indicator.*

canaries are monomorphic (both sexes look the same) you won't be able to tell which is which, so you have to rely on the honesty of the breeder or pet shop. Or you can watch a group of canaries closely and wait until one sings—a bird who sings is a male. You can tell a female either by DNA testing or if she lays an egg—then she's definitely a hen! Usually seasoned breeders are pretty good at being able to tell the genders apart.

You also might want to consider breed and color when you pair up your birds. Some mutations create very pretty offspring when paired. In addition, you need to know about the "lethal genes" so that you don't risk the death of part of the clutch of babies. Never breed two crested canaries together, and never breed two white canaries together. Also, it's a good idea to breed "hard feather" to "soft feather."

You also have to consider which birds are going to make the best parents. Some hens love to breed and rear young, and some aren't all that interested. The eager hen will probably make a better mother, so you have to keep an eye on your hens to see which ones are more the mothering type. Usually the good mother in the group will be the one actively building a nest and looking around for a mate.

## Breeding Supplies

Aside from the breeding cage, which can be the cage you keep one of the canaries in year round, you will need a nest and nesting material. You will find wire, wicker, and plastic nests. Many breeders don't like the wire and wicker nests because a toenail can easily become caught in them. Some breeders sew a soft pad or felt into the nest as a liner to prevent this. Nesting material can be anything from burlap to coco fiber to paper. Each hen will have a different preference, so offer a few choices.

## Breeding Condition

Canaries must be in tip-top shape to breed safely, especially the hen. She has to be strong, well nourished, and ready to undertake the stress of having eggs and rearing young. First, before breeding, your hen has to have spent time in a spacious cage where she could fly. She must be able to use her muscles to build the stamina she's going to need to breed and lay eggs. Also, a bird who flies has a stronger respiratory system, which can only serve to help her. Before she breeds, she has to be an athlete! It's likely that

FAMILY-FRIENDLY TIP

# Getting the Kids Involved

You child will no doubt marvel at the wonder of nature when you breed your canaries. It really is a miracle to see beautiful, whole, healthy canaries come from what was once an empty nest. The process of an egg turning into a bird is truly amazing and can teach a child some wonderful lessons. However, breeding canaries also can be fraught with tragedy and heartbreak, and that might not be something your young child is ready for. So either have a very frank conversation with your child about the risks of breeding your birds, or risk some tears and difficult questions if something does go wrong.

you're going to put the pair in a smaller cage to breed, so make sure that before you do so, the hen has had at least two or three months in the equivalent of a birdie mansion.

The next step in conditioning your pair is to feed them properly. Breeding pairs need to be fed the most nutritious meals possible before, during, and even after raising their chicks. Having eggs and raising young

*Your canaries, especially the hen, must be in top condition before you attempt to breed them.*

is very stressful, and diet plays a key role in whether or not the parents and the young will even make it through the season. Here are some conditioning tips:

- Increase the amount of protein that you offer the pair; a good egg food is perfect for this, and even some worms, if you can get your canary to take them (many will not).
- Increase the amount of leafy greens you offer, especially wet leafy greens in a shallow dish of water.
- Offer a shallow bath every day.
- Offer bee pollen and wheat germ a couple of times a week.
- Spirulina and nutritional yeast sprinkled over couscous is a great conditioning treat.
- Always offer a cuttlebone in the cage as a calcium source.
- Offer sprouted seed, a great source of vitamins and minerals.

When the eggs hatch, give the parents an overabundance of egg food, both homemade and commercially prepared. This protein source will help the babies grow— they need a lot of nutrients at this time. Rotate new food into the cage every couple of hours. Don't let any soft foods start to sour in the cage, or you risk losing the babies.

## Photosensitivity

Canaries, like many birds, are sensitive to the seasons, and their bodies react to when periods of light become shorter and longer. When the amount of daylight hours becomes longer in the spring, they instinctively know that it's breeding season, and they start to get ready to have babies. The male sings and courts the female, and she builds a nest. When the amount of light starts to become shorter after the summer solstice, the canary feels that it's time for a molt to replace old feathers with new ones. The male will usually stop singing at this time. Why should he sing? It's not breeding season anymore!

Many breeders manipulate their canaries using artificial lights. This is common practice. Not only does the light stimulate them to breed, it also can stop them from breeding when they need to rest. When you want to bring your birds into breeding mode, simply slowly increase the amount of daylight they receive, and by the time they are getting 11 hours, they will be ready to pair up. When they're getting 13 or 14 hours, they will be in full breeding mode. When you want them to take a rest, perhaps after two or three clutches (usually two), you can suddenly decrease their light to about nine hours again.

There are several ways to manipulate the light that your birds get. A simple way is just to cover the cage with a dark cloth, but that may put some birds off of breeding. A great way is to plug artificial sunlamps made for birds (full-spectrum bulbs) into timers and then put the birds into an otherwise dark room. Some people breed canaries in the basement so that they can control the light. If you're going to use this method, also put a nightlight or a blue lightbulb on a timer so that your canaries don't go from bright light to pitch darkness. You want to allow your hen time to get back to the nest before the lights go out for good.

Many canaries are at the whim of the household's comings and goings, where lighting is unpredictable, at best. People are up at night for a midnight snack, or holiday parties keep the birds up later than usual. These pet birds are constantly confused about what their bodies should be doing. Some individuals will nest in the middle of the winter or even begin a molt, which should actually take place in the summer. Everything is out of whack. Do your canary a favor and try to have some consistency with his lighting. Yes, you can manipulate your male canary into singing all year round or in the

## Canary Clubs

There are hundreds of canary clubs; in fact, there is probably one in your town or a town nearby. Each club is likely devoted to one type of canary, so check out various clubs to see which one suits you best. You will learn a lot by attending club meetings and shows and talking to other canary enthusiasts.

*Canaries normally lay about five eggs in a clutch. Their eggs are blue like a robins' but smaller.*

evening hours, but you are messing up his normal bodily clock, and it's unlikely that he'll live to see his golden years. Of course, allowing your canary to have natural light from a window and then letting him go to sleep when it's dark outside is a great way to keep him on nature's schedule.

## Breeding Timeline

Around the time that canaries start to notice that periods of light are getting longer—that spring is coming—is about the time when they start getting crabby with each other. With breeding season comes a boost of territoriality, especially from males. A group of canaries who may have been fairly peaceful during the winter will now squabble and even injure or kill each other. This is the time to separate your birds into peaceable pairs. Remember, if two canaries aren't a true breeding pair, they should not be housed together. Canaries like household activity, and they like to see other birds nearby, but they don't like to share their own space.

Once your male and female are showing interest in each other (he's singing to court her and she's making a nest), you can put them together in the same cage. Some breeding cages have a center divider so that the birds can see each other and have some interaction but not get to each other. This is a great way to observe them to make sure that they're going to get along. If they're kissing between the bars, they will probably get along when they're together. Also, you can just remove the center divider without stressing one of the birds by catching him and moving him to the breeding cage. There might be some fighting at first, so you have to keep an eye on them so that the male doesn't seriously injure the female. Many pairs will just get right down to business making a nest. Some hens make really elaborate, tall nests, and others are a little sloppy.

Some breeders will trim the feathers around the hen's vent (but not the actual vent feathers) to facilitate breeding, making it easier for the male to deposit his sperm. It's also a good idea to trim the nails at this time. Long nails can become trapped in the spaces in the nest, and the bird will either panic or not be able to leave the nest; you may think that she's sitting tight when she's actually trapped. Also, long nails can puncture and scramble the eggs.

Hens will lay about five eggs but can lay fewer or as many as eight in one clutch. The eggs are bluish in color. Most of the time, the hen will not start to incubate (sit on) the eggs until the last one is laid. This way, they will all hatch out at about the same time, one or two days apart. If she sat on them from the time the first egg was laid, they would be vastly different in age, and the smaller chicks wouldn't have a chance of surviving with older chicks in the nest. When the hen is sitting, she will rarely leave the nest. She relies on the male to feed her.

To tell if the eggs are fertile, you can "candle" them with a tool that looks like a flashlight on the end of a long,

## Showing Canaries

Most canary clubs hold a yearly show where you can bring your birds for exhibition. In many cases, you can only show a bird whom you have bred yourself. For song canaries, the show is a singing contest, usually done in teams. For color-bred and type canaries, the show is a beauty contest where contestants are judged based on how closely they resemble the standard for their breed.

*Canary eggs hatch about 14 days after the hen starts sitting on them.*

flexible neck. When the hen is out of the nest, gently place the head of the candler onto each egg and look for veins or a dark spot. If the egg is clear, wait a few more days to see if veins start to grow. Remove clear, unfertile eggs if you want your hen to lay others. If not, leave them under her until the other eggs hatch.

Eggs hatch in about 14 days from the time the hen starts "sitting tight," not from the time the first egg was laid. The chick is naked and looks a little like a wriggly alien, not the beautiful canary he will be in just a few weeks. Canary babies are "altricial," meaning that the young are blind and helpless and need careful parental care to survive. (This is in contrast to "precocial" animals, like ducks, that are relatively independent from the start.)

The chicks are fully feathered and leave the nest at about 18 days, although they will want to go back into the nest to sleep with their parents, and they still need to be fed. Some couples will get testy with the babies because they will want to go to nest again and won't want to deal with the intruding youngsters. This is the time to move them into another cage, usually when they are about a month old. Watch them for a few days to make sure that they are indeed eating on their own.

## Banding the Chicks

If you want to be able to permanently identify your chicks, show them, or sell them in certain states, you will have to band them. This means putting a small band on the leg that has a unique number and oftentimes other identifying marks, such as the breeder's initials and the state where the bird was bred. Most clubs sell either open (split) or closed bands. Closed bands must be put onto the leg when the babies are about a week old. It's not easy if you haven't done it before, so

*Hatchling canaries are blind, and helpless. They will depend completely on their parents for about 18 days.*

have an experienced person show you how before you try it yourself. And never, ever try to cut a band off by yourself! Have a veterinarian or an experienced breeder do it with a special tool. If you use anything other than this tool you will seriously hurt the bird.

## After Breeding Season

After breeding season, usually when you've allowed your pair to have two clutches of babies, you need to let them rest. Separate the male and female, preferably removing the male from her sight. Put them in spacious cages where they can fly and get some exercise. Feed them as if you were conditioning them for breeding season for a couple of weeks to bulk them up a bit after the stress of raising young.

## What Can Go Wrong

Some canary pairs aren't good parents. Perhaps the hen doesn't want to sit on the eggs, or she tosses the babies out of the nest. Sometimes she will lay a clutch of fertile eggs but then abandon the whole thing. What are you going to do in these cases? Most hobby breeders have other canaries nesting at the same time, so they will foster the eggs or the babies under other pairs that are better parents. If you don't have this option, you may have to try incubating the eggs and feeding the young yourself—no easy task with canaries, but it is often done.

Canary hens who aren't in good breeding condition, who have an underlying health issue, or who have bred too many times in succession can become egg bound. This means that she is unable to pass the egg because she is weak or the egg is malformed or even too soft due to a lack of calcium or other minerals in her body. This condition can be deadly for the hen if you don't catch the signs of it early enough. An egg-bound hen will not be as active as she was before. She will sit in the nest or at the bottom of the cage, usually panting and often puffed up. She may even become paralyzed.

If you suspect that your hen is egg bound, gently remove her from the cage and put her into a warm brooder or hospital cage at about 98° to 99°F (36.7° to 37.2°C). Make sure that she has water and food in the brooder or hospital cage. Put a few drops of olive oil into the opening of her vent (where the egg comes out). Don't push anything into the vent—just put the oil on the opening to lubricate the egg. If you can, put a drop of olive oil into her beak, too, but make sure that you don't aspirate (choke) her. Keep an eye on

## Fake Eggs

Fake canary eggs can be a lifesaver for a canary hen. Because you only want your canaries to raise two clutches a year (three at the maximum), you can prevent your hen from becoming depleted and exhausted by replacing her newly laid eggs with fake eggs. You should do this if she unexpectedly starts laying late in the season or lays so early that you know the timing suggests that by the end of the season she's going to be a wreck if she is allowed to raise too many youngsters. She will incubate these fake eggs for a couple of weeks, and then you can take them away from her. She will get to business then starting another clutch, and hopefully the timing will be right then, or if it's late in the season, you will just take away the nest and the male and she won't have the urge to lay more eggs.

*After leaving the nest, young canaries sleep with and are fed by their parents for a few days.*

her in the brooder, and call your veterinarian immediately. Egg binding usually requires medical attention. Once the egg has passed, place five fake canary eggs into her nest so that she thinks that she's done laying. These fake eggs will actually stop her from laying more, and she will start to sit on them.

## What Will You Do With the Babies?

If you're going to breed your canaries, keep in mind that you'll soon be overrun with birds if you don't find homes for them. Are you going to keep all of the babies? Remember that canaries aren't a social species, so you'll need separate cages or a large aviary if you're going to keep them together. If you're going to give them away, can you find good homes? If you're going to sell them, do you have a reputable place that will take your precious babies? These are just a few of the things you want to think about before you undertake the hobby breeding of any bird.

# Glossary

**agate:** A self-colored bird (*see* self) with diluted black and brown melanin (*see* melanin)

**blue:** A bird with a white ground color (*see* ground color) that has black and brown melanin (*see* melanin) present, creating the "blue" mutation

**buff:** A feather type that results
**cap:** The feathers on the crown of the bird's head

**cinnamon:** A cinnamon mutation lacks black pigmentation and has red eyes; on a white ground color, the bird is called "fawn"

**clear:** A clear bird has no markings among his feathers; he is just one color, either white, yellow, or buff

**cock:** A male bird

**color feeding:** Some canaries, like the red factor, can eat and drink certain chemicals—either man-made or naturally occurring—to enhance the color in their feathers. Color feeding is only done while the bird is molting and growing new feathers.

**dark:** A "dark" bird is one who shows pigmented variegation over 75 percent of his body

**dimorphic:** When the cock and the hen have a different physical appearance; in the canary, this happens in the mosaic mutation (*see* mosaic)

**factor:** Factors are the genes that create various feather colors, patterns, and structures in a bird

**fawn:** A white ground bird displaying cinnamon genes

**finish:** Orderliness and cleanliness in the bird's general appearance

**foul:** A heavily variegated bird

**foul tail:** White feathers in the tail

**foul wing:** White feathers in the wing

**frosted:** Buff feathers creating a bird with a white sheen over his ground color

**gene:** The factor in the bird's DNA that accounts for his characteristics

**green:** When a canary is showing both black and brown melanins; also called "normal" or "nominate"

**grizzle:** Ticking on the head; only considered grizzled when the ticking is on both sides of the head touching both eyes

**ground color:** The basic color of the body feathers, regardless of pigmented markings

**hen:** A female bird

**hot color:** Profound, rich color

**ino:** Referring to a genetic mutation that strips melanin from the feathers and makes the eyes pink

**line breeding:** When breeders pair closely related birds (usually parent to offspring or sibling to sibling) to enhance genetic effects and obtain desirable characteristics

**marking:** Referring to variegation or ticking on a bird (*see* ticking and variegation)

**melanin:** Pigmentation; in the canary, either dark black or brown or lighter shades of black or brown

**melodiousness:** The harmonic tones in a bird's song; the flow and stream of the song

**mosaic:** A sex-linked gene in the mosaic canary causes it to be dimorphic, meaning that there's a visual difference between the genders; the feather quality is frosted

**mutation:** A bird with different physical characteristics than the "nominate" or "normal" coloration or patterning

**nest feather:** A bird who has not had his first molt

**normal:** A "green" canary, one who has both black and brown melanin

**outcross:** Pairing unrelated birds

**patchy:** When the color is uneven, often occurring in Red Factor canaries due to inexperienced color feeding

**range:** The lowest and highest notes in a bird's song

**rendition:** The evaluation of a canary's song or entire performance

**self** or **self-colored:** A dark bird who shows none of his ground color because he is highly variegated

**ticking:** A single mark anywhere on the body

**tone:** Musicality regarding pitch, strength, and quality

**tour:** A canary's entire song

**variegated:** Melanin pigmentation anywhere on the bird's body

# Resources

## Organizations

### American Federation of Aviculture
P.O.Box 7312
N. Kansas City, MO 64116
Telephone: (816) 421-3214
Fax: (816)421-3214
E-mail: afaoffice@aol.com
www.afabirds.org

### American Norwich Society
P.O. Box 35973
Las Vegas, NV 89133
www.angelfire.com/fl/norwichcanary

### American Waterslager Society
Tom Trujillo, President
556 S. Cactus Wren Street
Gilbert, AZ 85296
Telephone: (480) 892-5464
www.waterslagers.com/text/
contacts.htm

### Avicultural Society of America
PO Box 5516
Riverside, CA 92517-5516
Telephone: (951) 780-4102
Fax: (951) 789-9366
E-mail: info@asabirds.org
www.asabirds.org

### Aviculture Society of the United Kingdom
Arcadia-The Mounts-East Allington-Totnes
Devon TQ9 7QJ
United Kingdom
E-mail: admin@avisoc.co.uk
www.avisoc.co.uk

### International Columbus Fancy Association
Robert Wild, Secretary
305 Grosvenor Court
Boilingbrook, IL 60440
Telephone: (630) 985-4416
E-mail: R.Wild@comcast.net
www.angelfire.com/wv2/columbus-fancy

### International Gloster Breeders Association
Regina McCarthy
58 Joanne Drive
Hanson, MA 02341
E-mail: TheBirdBreeder@aol.com
www.igbaglostersusa.com

### National Gloster Club
Cheryl Cardona, NGC Secretary
12 South Meadow
Woodbury, CT 06798
Telephone: (203) 263-0014
Fax: (203) 263-6270
www.nationalglosterclub.org

## Oakland International Roller Canary Club

Steve Billmire, Show Manager
38341 Anita Court
Fremont, CA
Telephone: (510) 794-6719
E-mail: oircc@comcast.net
www.geocities.com/Heartland/8813

## Santa Clara Valley Canary and Exotic Bird Club

PO Box 3466
Santa Clara, CA 95055-3466
E-mail: scvcebc@yahoo.com
www.geocities.com/SiliconValley/1570/index.html

## Stafford Canary Club of America

Tom Ressel, President or
Carl Biers, Vice President
851 Neptune Street
Port Charles, FL 33948
E-mail: tomressel@yahoo.com
www.staffords-usa.com/

## Yorkshire Canary Club of America

1210 Ivy Road
Manasquan, NJ 08738
E-mail: truiz47@comcast.net
www.yorkshirecanary.com/index2.html

## Emergency Resources

### ASPCA Animal Poison Control Center

Telephone: (888) 426-4435
E-mail: napcc@aspca.org (for non-emergency, general information only)
http:////www.apcc.aspca.org

### Bird Hotline

P.O. Box 1411
Sedona, AZ 86339-1411
E-mail: birdhotline@birdhotline.com
http:////www.birdhotline.com/

## Rescue AND Adoption Organizations

### American Humane Association (AHA)

63 Inverness Drive East
Englewood, CO 80112
Telephone: (303) 792-9900
Fax: 792-5333
www.americanhumane.org

### American Society for the Prevention of Cruelty to Animals (ASPCA)

424 E. 92$^{nd}$ Street
New York, NY 10128-6804
Phone: (212) 876-7700
http://www.aspca.org

**Best Friends Animal Sanctuary**
5001 Angel Canyon Road
Kanab, UT 84741-5001
Phone: (435) 644-2001
info@bestfriends.org
http://www.bestfriends.com/

**Bird Placement Program**
P.O. Box 347392
Parma, OH, 44134-7392
Phone: (330) 772-1627 or (216)
749-3643
www.avi-sci.com/bpp/

**Caged Bird Rescue**
911 Thomson Road
Pegram, TN 37143
Phone: (615) 646-3949

**Exotic Bird Rescue Ring**
http://www.neebs.org/birdresc.htm

**Feathered Friends Adoption and
Rescue Program**
East Coast Headquarters
4751 Ecstasy Circle
Cocoa, FL, 32926
Phone: (407) 633-4744
West Coast Branch
Phone: (941) 764-6048
http://members.aol.com/_ht_a/MA
Horton/FFAP.html

**The Fund for Animals**
200 West 57th Street
New York, NY 10019
Phone: (212) 246-2096
fundinfo@fund.org

**Northcoast Bird Adoption and
Rehabilitation Center, Inc.
(NBARC)**
P.O. Box 367
Aurora, OH
Phone: (330) 425-9269 or (330)
562-6999
www.adoptabird.com

**Royal Society for the Prevention
of Cruelty to Animals (RSPCA)**
Telephone: 0870 3335 999
Fax: 0870 7530 284
www.rspca.org.uk

**Tucson Avian Rescue and
Adoption (TARA)**
Phone: (520) 531-9305 or (520)
322-9685
www.found-pets.org/tara.html

Canary

## Veterinary Resources

**Association of Avian Veterinarians**
P.O. Box 811720
Boca Raton, FL 33481-1720
Telephone: (561) 393-8901
Fax: (561) 393-8902
E-mail: AAVCTRLOFC@aol.com
www.aav.org

## Internet Resources

**American Singer Canary Homepage**
www.americansingercanary.com

**American Singer's Club**
www2.upatsix.com/asc/

**Exotic Pet Vet.Net**
www.exoticpetvet.net

**A Place for Canaries**
www.robirda.com/

**Old Variety Canary Association**
www.ovca.us

**United Spanish Timbrado Fanciers**
www.spanishtimbrado.us/Home_Page.php

## Magazines

*Bird Talk*
3 Burroughs
Irvine, CA 92618
Telephone: 949-855-8822
Fax: (949) 855-3045
http://www.birdtalkmagazine.com

*Bird Times*
7-L Dundas Circle
Greensboro, NC 27407
Telephone: (336) 292-4247
Fax: (336) 292-4272
E-mail: info@petpublishing.com
http://www.birdtimes.com

*Good Bird*
PO Box 684394
Austin, TX 78768
Telephone: 512-423-7734
Fax: (512) 236-0531
E-mail: info@goodbirdinc.com
www.goodbirdinc.com

# Index

Canary

111

Index

## About the Author

Avian Care and Behavior Consultant, Nikki Moustaki, is the author of 22 books on birds and bird behavior and works regularly with clients to help heal the relationship between them and their birds.

She has written for many national magazines, as well as having been featured on television and radio shows. She has been involved with birds since 1988 when she became active in local bird clubs, and began breeding and showing birds. During those first few years, she kept lovebirds, cockatiels, budgies, lories, macaws, Amazons, conures, finches, canaries, and *Brotergeris*. Around 1993, Nikki became aware of the bird overpopulation problem, stopped breeding birds, and began helping in rescue efforts. Today, she lives with an African Grey parrot, a Meyer's parrot, lovebirds, and two schnauzers, and she hosts www.goodbird.com. and www.birdfessions.com